SHAWN MICALLEF

THE TROUBLE WITH BRUNCH

WORK, CLASS AND THE PURSUIT OF LEISURE

COACH HOUSE BOOKS, TORONTO

 Canada Council   Conseil des Arts
for the Arts   du Canada    ONTARIO ARTS COUNCIL
CONSEIL DES ARTS DE L'ONTARIO   Canadä

Published with the generous assistance of the Canada Council for the Arts and the Ontario Arts Council. Coach House Books also acknowledges the support of the Government of Canada through the Canada Book Fund and the Government of Ontario through the Ontario Book Publishing Tax Credit.

LIBRARY AND ARCHIVES CANADA CATALOGUING IN PUBLICATION

Micallef, Shawn, 1974-, author
    The trouble with brunch : work, class and the pursuit of leisure / Shawn Micallef.

(Exploded views)
Issued in print and electronic formats.
ISBN 978-1-55245-285-1 (pbk.).

    1. Leisure--Social aspects. 2. Social classes. I. Title.

GV14.45.M53 2014   306.4'81   C2013-904745-X

The Trouble with Brunch is available as an ebook: ISBN 978 1 77056 365 0.

Purchase of the print version of this book entitles you to a free digital copy. To claim your ebook of this title, please email sales@chbooks.com with proof of purchase or visit chbooks.com/digital. (Coach House Books reserves the right to terminate the free download offer at any time.)

To Windsor, Ontario,
a good place to come from

A Tale of Two Brunches

Few leisure pursuits enjoy the near-religious devotion that brunch does. In cities around the world, it's a weekly ritual that can take up an entire day, with its devotees chattering, texting, tweeting and Instagramming about the lineup, the food, the decor, the experience. One must brunch in order to live – or so the passions involved would suggest. Somewhere, in his writing about the good life, Aristotle must have a lost chapter on brunch. But scratch the surface of brunch (maybe with your grapefruit spoon), and you'll find a high-pressure, predictably choreographed event that consumes time and money most people can't afford to waste. The overpriced food is overthought and overrated, the service often substandard. It's a grand performance of leisure that is not, in itself, at all leisurely.

Most of the brunches I've endured in my lifetime have taken place in Toronto, but I've also been to brunch in New York, Montreal, London, Buenos Aires and a few other cities in between. Though the locations varied, as did the people I ate with, the elements of each meal recurred in such ways that an event that's often billed as unique, local and authentic took on the unsurprising uniformity of a Starbucks outlet – the chairs, tables, display cases and washrooms all the same, just rearranged a little from location to location. Empathy, I observed, does not exist at brunch. Diners linger over cooling, almost empty cups of Lapsang souchong even as people waiting for a table stand in conspicuous view. There is no inclination to clear out and let others enjoy their time here. Brunchers treat servers uncharitably and servers, in turn, view them with contempt. Chefs bury the dregs of the week's dinners under rich sauces, arranging them in curious combinations. At on-trend brunch restaurants, heretofore liberal-minded, compassionate and socially aware people become monstrous amalgams of Ayn Rand and Margaret Thatcher: there is no society, no community – there are only small, awkwardly shaped tables and the individuals seated uncomfortably around them.

In Windsor, Ontario, where I grew up, the codes and rituals of brunch were different. So different, in fact, that the two kinds of brunches should not even share a name. Windsor is a midwestern, industrial (or, perhaps, post-industrial) city across the river from Detroit. It's a Springsteen kind of town, dominated by the car industry, but thanks to the Canadian social safety net, not nearly as desperate as the dying landscapes described in the Boss's lyrics. Brunch in Windsor was a rare event, attended only on Easter, Mother's Day or after a christening or First Communion. Often held at an Italian or Croatian banquet hall, a golf course dining hall or one of the fancier hotel restaurants, brunch meant a buffet with a long line of metal warming pans over a lit Sterno can with the strange blue flame that signalled to kids (and maybe some adults) it was a special occasion. *Fire in a can!* The brunch lines moved quickly and efficiently. People served themselves until they reached the end of the buffet, where someone in a chef's hat would carve and serve slices of roast beef, while referring to everyone, even us preteens, as *sir* or *ma'am*. It was quite a thrill. Certain airs were put on, but obviously and without shame. Seating was at a large table. Nobody's arms, knees or elbows touched. Larger groups were seated immediately. Washrooms were plentiful, toilets worked on the first flush and the hand dryers were powerful. There was always a wide variety of traditional breakfast and dinner items available, but there was no inappropriately creative mingling of foods. Separate but equal, the scrambled eggs stayed in the eggs pan, and the roast potatoes, green peas, chicken legs and pancakes all remained in their own respective pans. If you combined two things that weren't supposed to go together and gave this concoction an obnoxious name, you'd probably be asked to leave. There was camaraderie at these brunches, conversations had and joy shared, but the food remained, at its core, fuel for doing other things.

In 2000, when I moved to Toronto, I was often invited to brunch. And as a newcomer, I felt compelled to go. These brunches were served in tiny, fashionably fey places carved out of old butcher shops, Victorian houses or former five-and-dimes with enough intact sandblasted architectural details and artifacts to remind customers of the dirty, laborious days we have left behind, a nod to a workaday world that has become leisurely. There was always a lineup, even if the diner down the street had free booths and identical food. Even then, brunch was a significant part of the rise of 'extreme eating' – the proliferation and celebration of unhealthy (usually meat-heavy) foods, meals and restaurants that appeared along a hollandaise-to-charcuterie continuum. 'I love the smell of maple bacon in the morning!' brunchers might have shouted. The ritual intake of fat and grease at brunch (often devoured as a supposed hangover remedy) took on a defiantly rebellious air, akin to teenagers wearing punk T-shirts to school, affluent white people using hip-hop slang or investment bankers donning leathers and riding perfectly polished Harleys on weekends. The unhealthiness of the food was, perversely, value-added. The thicker and more fatty the hollandaise, the greater the risk for people who otherwise led very safe, secure lives. By the same token, the small portions and extortionate prices added a patina of preciousness – *Look how much I'm paying for food that's bad for me and doesn't even fill me up.*

I went, because that's what I thought I was supposed to do. After a number of these extended, uncomfortable meals, I realized that even though I liked the people I was with, brunch was not an enjoyable way to be with them. At the same time, during the misery of these meals, regretfully aware that the sugary buzz of my mimosa would likely make the rest of the day a write-off, brunch provided me with a particularly vivid prism through which to view class and leisure in the West. Why were my fellow brunchers, most of them working longer hours than their parents' generation had, and often for less money, squandering their precious free time on something as onerous as this chronically unsatisfying midday meal? With so much of modern life in unending flux, I wondered what the way the contemporary, urban middle class spends its leisure time could tell us about who they are and how they see themselves. And further – are there other delusional fictions the middle class tells itself about its lifestyle that are allowing for erosions of quality of life? The line between leisure and work is increasingly blurred, and the notion of working nine to five seems archaically quaint now. If what's thought of as leisure time well-spent is, in fact, not spent well at all, what does this mean? And why was I coming across similar brunch scenes when I travelled to what I thought were different cultures, and could that sameness be useful in connecting people in disparate places?

The artifice and performance of leisure around brunch and other non-work activities has created a smokescreen that clouds our understanding of our work, social and civic lives. A lack of class-based self-examination means we may have been brunching while Aristotle's elusive good life has, in fact, slipped away. Without a clear-eyed look at how class functions in our lives, whether it's how we view the neighbourhoods we live in, or where we shop for food, it becomes easy to forget the hypocrisies that infect and threaten middle-class ideals. The brunching class needs a class-consciousness reset, one that will allow us to understand how we live now, not how we *think* we live. The fierce individualism that creative producers require to make their unique works doesn't have to be a solo pursuit; connections and collaborations can be made to shore up the foundations of this new emerging class just as the working class did throughout the twentieth century. There's more in common among these workers than not, but these similarities aren't as obvious as they were in the past. The trouble with brunch is it could be so much more.

As a relative newcomer to the so-called middle class, I've had the privilege of experiencing it with a context I might not have if I'd been raised in a self-consciously middle-class environment. In Windsor, I always thought of myself as middle-class, though I recognize now that many of the signifiers of my life were working-class. At least, that's what they're considered by the middle class outside of cities like Windsor. Springsteen towns offer considerable perspective on how contemporary life in larger, mixed-economy cities play out. When I arrived in Toronto, I became part of a culture – semi-bohemian, creative, academic, artistic, intellectual, call it what you will – that was ostensibly middle-class and enjoyed middle-class pursuits like brunch, but that, if you define middle-class strictly by income levels, was hardly middle-class at all. In Windsor, I knew people who worked at the Chrysler plant and who could afford to buy a home with a two- or three-car garage before their twenty-fifth birthdays. In Toronto, I hardly knew anyone who owned even a five-hundred-square-foot condo.

That has changed, of course, even in Windsor. While the city remains defiantly attached to its manufacturing and industrial roots, it is also undergoing gentrification in its own minor key. There are hip bike shops, indie bars, bookstores run by iconoclast literary presses. There are even brunch spots where you won't see a can of Sterno but you'll find vegan entrées made from local Essex County produce and, yes, artisanal bacon and fair-trade coffee. Such gentrification – often seen as desirable and courted in places like Windsor – is unfolding in post-industrial cities all across the continent, from Hamilton to Pittsburgh, St. Louis to St. John's. As traditional industrial and resource economies falter, these metropolises are now trying desperately to diversify their economies through entrepreneurial innovation, tech, tourism and a vast array of cultural endeavours that, broadly, fall under a new classification known as the creative class.

This shift isn't always successful, and in many cases the gentrification has brought along unsurprising problems of affordability and homogeneity. But it's having radical ramifications for our understanding of class. How does this new creative class interact with what we traditionally perceive as the lower, middle and upper classes? Are these categories still useful, and if so, for what purpose? For my part, when I moved to Toronto, I found myself directly confronting an existential dilemma. I was suddenly trying to 'pass' as middle class by grasping at a sensibility I knew mostly through the movies and books. This is certainly not an Eliza Doolittle story – the changes I went through were much more subtle and even began in Windsor when I went to university and decided to continue on to grad school – but never underestimate how overwhelming and vertiginous it is to realize, during a social situation, that you're ostensibly from a rung or two lower than someone else, when the things and experiences people around you are talking about suddenly seem foreign. During conversations, there were many knowing nods on my part, when I pretended to understand and agree, only to Google, when no one was looking, the unfamiliar references and names – Negri, Žižek, Arendt –

that were being casually dropped in conversation. 'Of course I know what Gramsci thought about hegemony,' I'd say, 'but I must pop out to the washroom right now, and yes, I do need to take my phone in there with me.' Sometimes the references were academic, other times literary, musical – no, I don't have a favourite opera, but does *Fantasia* count? – or even around matters of social etiquette. Both 'high' and 'low' culture were part of the community I aspired to join, but my major in the university of life had heretofore focused mainly on the latter. None of this was, or is, terribly onerous – Wikipedia is a class-jumping grifter's best friend – but it takes a quick learner, and not everybody has the patience or desire to do this.

Why did I even want to be middle-class? In a word, it's incredibly attractive. The ideal middle-class life takes the edge off Hobbes' infamously dire characterization of the state of nature. In the middle-class ideal, there is the possibility of a so-called work-life balance, where work is fulfilling, performed largely by choice rather than necessity, and life includes ample time for worthwhile leisure and socializing. Above all, the middle class represented a solid foundation upon which to build a life, one where I could have some control and agency over my own destiny, rather than accepting the reflexive non-choice so many of my fellow Windsorites accepted – a life of reasonably well-paid, if increasingly precarious, factory work. However, now that I'm here, essentially ensconced in the middle-class life I thought I had dreamed of, I'm worried I too might become confused about what being middle-class means and thus oblivious to its shortcomings, blind spots and pitfalls.

Figuring out what class means is a work-in-progress for me, and this slim volume is, in part, an attempt at articulating the shift I went through over the last decade and a half, as my circumstances changed (even if my income level didn't come along for the ride). This is not an exhaustive study of class and class shifts; people with different racial, economic or gender backgrounds will have a difference experience of class than I did, some considerably more fraught than mine. But I want to understand class because it's been there all my life, and most of the time, I didn't notice. It's only because I've moved between the classes that I see it now, the elephant in so many rooms.

We don't talk about class in North America very much – unless we're saying, proudly, how we don't have a class system. Or, unless you're a vote-seeking politician vaguely, unhelpfully talking about the 'disappearing middle class.' Similarly, in the U.K. we hear a lot about how the class system no longer exists. And yet it does, all around us. It exists in sensibility, in lifestyle, in income. The only people who think class doesn't exist are ensconced deep within a bubble of their own class, unable to see where it ends. All of these things, especially income, make us incredibly uncomfortable when discussed and unwrapped. (Perhaps this is why TV shows and magazine articles about real estate are so popular – they're a covert surrogate for an actual, open discussion of class.)

We need to talk more about class, both to understand our relationship to our selves and others, and to examine why we can't seem to find the same sense of unity as working classes did and do. But also, and most significantly, to see what kind of illusions we've created about the good life that seemingly surrounds us.

From the Factory Floor
to the Brunch Table

In the sixth or seventh grade, a friend's mom was giving me a ride home and, as I began to tell her which house was mine, mentioning the recently paved, double-wide driveway, she cut me off: 'I know which one is yours. We all know who's got the big new paved driveway.' Even among the same class, there is ample room for these kinds of subtle and, yes, concrete status markers. Her tone wasn't mean, but it wasn't exactly friendly either, and the remark suggested that our family had achieved something others in the neighbourhood hadn't, and that driveways had some status associated with them. The subsection of our suburban-nearly-exurban area contained a lot of first-generation Italian and Croatian immigrants, and being a partially Maltese family, ours fell into a bit of a mixed ethnic clique. Many of the men in the families around us were either general labourers or in skilled trades, and installing a concrete or interlocking brick driveway was a routine activity on a warm weekend day. We were quite friendly with our Croatian next-door neighbours – he a General Motors line worker, she a hairdresser with a home shop – and when they had their driveway done, we did ours too, sharing their Croatian crew, most of them friends and acquaintances who did this stuff on the side, either pro bono or for much less than a contractor would charge. Some of our relatives came over to help too, turning a home-improvement project that might be completely contracted out into a quasi-DIY exercise, reducing the cost of what still was an expensive endeavour.

That's how Windsor worked and, to a large extent, still works. Everybody knows somebody who knows how to do something, whether paving a driveway or changing the brake rotors on a car. When my mom needs the kitchen faucet fixed she'll call a fellow named Camille who is part of that Croatian clique, but is also the husband of a woman who worked with my mom at GM. Even now, when I'm visiting at Christmas, she'll ask if anything is wrong with the sixteen-year-old Chrysler I drive – our now-retired neighbour and his buddy do car repairs in their garage in their spare time. They can make me feel like I'm a teenager again, as they bossily send me out to buy the specific windshield-washer pump they say I need. But the labour is 80 percent cheaper than if I were to have the work done in Toronto, where I don't know anyone who can fix a car.

Our driveway was paved in 1986. Times were good. After taking a decade off to raise my sister and me, Mom had gone back to work the year before. She had hit the Windsor jackpot with that job at GM, which had even more closely linked Mom and our neighbour, as well as our households – both were now tethered to the prosperity of the same company. Windsor is the little Motor City: the three dominant American car companies in Detroit all built subsidiary plants on the Canadian side of the river, partially the result of the Auto Pact, a 1965 agreement that ensured car production remained in Canada that was in force until 1994, when the North American Free Trade Agreement changed the rules. These were, once upon a time, the 'good money' jobs – jobs for life. Jobs that had benefits that often propelled people firmly into the middle class, economically speaking. The ones that are left are still good money jobs, though few people have faith they're for life. Even then, in the mid-1980s, Mom's union wage hovered around $20 an hour; it was a long way from the small village in Nova Scotia where she was born and that she left at eighteen because the fishery there sometimes had work but often didn't. She left that village reluctantly, but the change was dramatic. When she moved to Windsor in 1966, the city was a prosperous boomtown that, like present-day Calgary, drew a steady migration from Atlantic Canada. In Windsor, good blue- or white-collar jobs could be found quickly, and didn't require a post-secondary education. Mom's first and, other than GM, only other job in Ontario was at the local public utility provider, a position she found by simply walking into the human resources office and asking if they were hiring. Though entry-level, it came with a full pension and the expectation that, if she wanted to, she could remain there for the rest of her working life.

Also seeking work, Dad had emigrated to Windsor two years earlier, but from much farther afield. Malta in the mid-1960s, twenty years after taking a beating in the war, was an austere place with few prospects for a new high school graduate. My grandparents took advantage of a free ride on a chartered plane sponsored by the Maltese and Canadian governments, direct from Malta to Toronto, and arrived within months of the Beatles landing at JFK. The two events are tangled together in my imagination and I've always pictured thousands of people at the Toronto airport's brand-new and fantastically modern Aeroquay One greeting my relatives as they stepped off the plane. The program that brought them here is unimaginable today, but this was a moment when one country had a surplus population and the other needed immigrants to feed its wildly growing economy.

Detroit was my father's family's ultimate destination, as there were some Maltese connections there, but Windsor was easier to get to due to Commonwealth openness, and the plan was to wait there until they could move to the States. But soon, my grandfather got a job at Chrysler, and my father, after a few odd jobs at various companies, landed in the mailroom at Hiram Walker, the distillery that makes Canadian Club Whisky and, along with the auto companies, is one of Windsor's biggest and most stable employers, with similarly high wages. My grandparents purchased their own home within a year of moving to Windsor, something they were unable to afford in Malta, and Detroit was forgotten. Dad's is also an old story, of someone rising through the ranks from the most entry of entry-level jobs, through accounting and into middle management. For years he worked in industrial relations, negotiating union contracts and dealing with grievances and arbitration until his final promotion to a shift manager in the plant, overseeing the employees draining and filling the whisky barrels. Like many Hiram Walker families, we had two planters in the yard made from a sawed-in-half whisky barrel that could no longer hold its liquor, but did well with soil.

I didn't much think about class in Windsor but for the vague notion that I was part of the middle class. There was little reason to think about it at all, though – it wasn't often we noticed there even *were* other classes. There were certainly some people who had more money, and others who were poor, and driveways that were paved with asphalt and others with concrete, but in a heavily unionized area of around 250,000 people, there was a sense that everyone was on roughly the same level because so many people got to participate in its wealth. Windsor was attractive because of its prosperity, but also because that prosperity gave it an economic equilibrium.

While in middle management, my father was often in direct opposition to those on the labour side, but there was something about the way Windsor worked, and in particular Hiram Walker, that smoothed over the adversarial nature of that relationship. Knowing that the ultimate outcome of labour negotiations would likely be reasonable – that's how the system tended to work – there was a kind of solidarity. Dad recounts that, after bitter arbitration sessions, with opposing parties yelling accusations, insults and profanity at each other, both sides would retire to the Victoria Tavern for drinks. The Old Vic was, and is, a cross between a dive bar and an old-school pub; it attracted everyone, no matter the colour of their collar. Windsor has many of these places. When my dad and his co-workers met there, tensions and conflict from the boardroom were left behind; the arguments, accusations and swearing were just part of the system, the motions they went through in their various roles. Outside, they were all of the same place, regardless of the relatively minor differences in income. People within the company socialized together (there were a few inter-company social clubs), played on the same sports teams together (Dad organized the company baseball team and both white- and blue-collar workers all wore matching Walker hats and uniforms) and visited each other's homes. When we were young, we were taken along, sometimes to an executive's home, other times to a line worker's. The distinction between the two didn't exist until I was much older and started to pay attention to formal hierarchies and read Marxist political theory in university. As employees' children, we had many of our extracurricular activities determined by the company too. I bowled in a Saturday-morning Hiram Walker youth league for a decade, and played in a company hockey league, even curled and golfed one season, respectively. The kids playing, and the parents coaching and watching, occupied a comparable range of positions on the economic ladder, but there was no evidence of class tensions or social hierarchy.

When there were intimations of class, they tended to be extreme. One year we bought a used Commodore 64 computer from the adult son of the then-owner of Hiram Walker, himself a vice-president of the company. He lived in a large house on Riverside Drive. Running along the Detroit River, with fantastic views of the namesake city to the north, 'the Drive' is one of the few parts of Windsor that's conspicuously upper-class, at least in terms of property values. The combination of location and job title was vivid enough to make me aware that this family was from a different rung of society. But Windsor being Windsor, for a time in the 1980s my mom also went to an exercise class with his wife. And, apart from a few exceptions, everyone went to the same mall and the same restaurants, and sent their kids to the same public schools. The Drive itself wasn't all traditional elites either, as many rank-and-file autoworkers owned riverfront properties (though it remains the street on which you will mostly likely find Conservative lawn signs during an election). A number of the larger and more conspicuous homes were new money, purchased by tool-and-die kings, guys who were as working-class as any Chrysler assembly-line employee but who had capitalized on the automotive economy and successfully started their own shops, feeding the industry and eventually buying big houses.

Still, everybody mixed.

Boomtowns always go bust. By the 1970s and 1980s, the jobs in Windsor weren't as plentiful as they had been in the mid-1960s. If you had one of the 'good jobs,' there was a sense, in those decades, that this was your one and only shot at it, a very different feeling from when my parents arrived in the city – then there were always more jobs should you ever want another. If anything, that feeling has only intensified in recent years, and this was made more explicit when I returned home one Christmas eight years after I left for Toronto. At a party at a friend's house, I met a woman my age who had finished university at the same time but who had taken a very different path. While I went to grad school, graduated and moved away, she was hired at the Ford plant, where her father worked, though she had earned a BA during this time too.

This is a common story in Windsor, of people going to university but ending up with a job in one of the local factories. Chrysler, in particular, had a scheme called TPT – temporary part-time. These were weekend or midnight-shift and vacation-replacement jobs that were especially plentiful when the massive factory that produced the company-saving minivan was going 24/7. It was a job that the children of employees often got when they were just out of high school or going to university. Whenever I see a Chrysler minivan on the road today, it's like bumping into an old friend, as I know the people who built parts of it. These were the kids who were able to buy their own Dodge trucks, Chevy Camaros and Ford Mustangs (there were two models: a forgettable one with four cylinders, and the legendary one with a 5.0-litre eight-cylinder engine, the one Vanilla Ice spoke of so highly in his hit from the same era, 'Ice Ice Baby').

I got to experience this a bit myself. The week after high school graduation, I found myself on steady afternoons in the Hiram Walker bottling room, a place that looked very much like the Milwaukee brewery line seen in the opening credits of *Laverne & Shirley*. I did a bunch of jobs there: feeding empty bottles onto the line, putting full bottles into boxes, stacking boxes on pallets and sometimes scraping misapplied labels off bottles and affixing new ones by hand. To this day I can't walk through a liquor store without looking closely at Canadian Club bottles to see if the labels are on correctly. I sometimes left at the end of our shift at midnight drenched in whisky after one of the fillers burst an O-ring or a bottle I grabbed shattered in my hand.

A few dozen of us were hired that summer, just as the recession of the early 1990s was dissipating. Some, like me, were employee relatives, others were not. Though my father had been in management, I don't recall any disrespect ever being thrown our way, as some of the nepotism extended to rank-and-file employees as well. We immediately became part of the factory-floor family, even shown the special locker that contained the stash of airplane booze bottles (there was a mini-line that filled the mini-bottles – working in a distillery presents both temptation and addiction issues). That summer I learned new swear words, went to the Old Vic after work for a quick round of draft beer and saw how union politics worked (I received my very own Canadian Auto Workers card, something so many of my immediate and extended family and friends have had at one time or another), and came to understand the toll repetitive physical work takes on a body, even a nineteen-year-old one.

As our day of seniority approached – the point sixty days in, before the full protection of the union kicks in, when an employer can let you go without cause – a handful of us were asked to stay on. I was about to start university, but the nineteen dollars an hour I was making was intoxicating. My previous job had been delivering newspapers, so the pay jump was radical (and it would be nearly two decades before I made more than that). I dropped an afternoon class that conflicted with the job and spent the next few months attending school by day and working in the factory from 3:30 p.m. until midnight. Fifteen- or sixteen-hour days. Although I knew I had to go to school, I also could not quit this job. Nobody in Windsor would quit a job like this.

Had Hiram Walker not laid me off two months into university, and I'd instead somehow been able to work there and earn my degree at the same time without burning out, I might have worked at the factory indefinitely and stayed in Windsor. I'd have bought a house and a new car. Instead, apart from those first two months, I spent much of my university days working for minimum wage at a not particularly cool record shop in the local mall. Before I retired from the music industry and moved to Toronto, I was making seven dollars an hour, fifteen cents over what was then minimum wage. Working at the mall, I saw most of the city pass through, from company presidents to line workers. Like many North American cities, the mall replaced downtown as a shopping and social nexus, and in a mid-size city like Windsor there was only one regional mall. (When I return home now, I usually make a trip there just to walk, as it's the only place you can see Windsorites walking around en masse in public, and maybe bump into old friends.) While I was working there during grad school, some of my professors would occasionally come in, and I felt what I now recognize as a twinge of class consciousness – it embarrassed me a bit to work a mall-rat job while writing papers on postmodern international relations theory. Silly, really, as there was never any indication that anyone even gave a second thought to my work there, but for the first time I felt like something was changing.

I was the first member of my family to go to grad school, and while I didn't face any real opposition to the decision, there were questions about what I would do with a master's degree in political science. While my parents were supportive, my nana, perhaps more honestly, asked why I didn't get a trade, referring to Maltese friends of the family whose sons had gone into tool-and-die or become electricians and were making, at age twenty-three, almost thirty dollars an hour. My response – that I liked studying, that I didn't want to pursue a trade – fell on deaf, unsympathetic ears. Her experience in both Malta and Windsor taught my grandmother that following one's dream or interests was a shrewd strategy. The only right and logical thing to do was take the quickest route to a well-paid job. Better yet, one that was unionized, with all the attendant benefits that came with membership. I've got relatively straight teeth now thanks to years of wearing retainers and braces, an orthodontic state sometimes called a 'Buzz Hargrove smile,' named after the then-head of the Canadian Auto Workers union who negotiated generous benefits packages for employees and their families. There was no guarantee of straight teeth following the path I was undertaking. And as I watched my contemporaries buy homes at early ages – those in the general labour rank-and-file bought smaller ones while the skilled tradesmen sometimes built new, oversized homes in the subdivisions on the edge of town – self-doubt crept in. Was I making the right decision? It was disconcerting to watch people establish their lives while I was gambling on an unknown future. The only thing I knew for certain was that I would have to leave Windsor when I was finished school – both because I wanted to and because there was little I could do there unless I stayed and played the job lottery.

So, when my new friend at that Christmas party began to tell me her story, I understood her decision to take an immediate job at Ford rather than hunting for the more elusive job a university degree might make possible. She settled in, bought a house and let life carry on. The problem was, after a decade and a half working there, she had just been laid off during the downturn that occurred in 2008. Worried about how she would afford her mortgage and other expenses, she started crying. Ford had consumed and wasted her life, she said. She wanted to be a photographer, a long-held dream and something she did in her spare time. It was jarring to be at a festive party and then have the woman I was speaking to become suddenly inconsolable. I tried to convince her that her life, in fact, was not over and that people I'd met in Toronto changed careers all the time, sometimes with 180-degree shifts. She nodded, but I don't think she believed me. Job mobility was not common in Windsor. Few people changed careers once or twice, never mind the half-dozen or more times people do so now. In Windsor, if you were laid off, you waited and hoped to be called back, safe for the time being in the unemployment-insurance safety net. There was little else to do; another job was perhaps a possibility, but not a career shift.

My leaving Windsor then also meant getting away from the precariousness of this boom-and-bust economy, of knowing not that the bottom *could* fall out from underneath you at some point, but that it *will*. Living in Windsor is like living in Los Angeles: you are always waiting for the big one in a state of calm awareness. I didn't recognize it while I lived there, but an instinctive understanding of this is inherent to a working-class sensibility. It might even be its defining characteristic. Life goes on, plans are made, families raised, homes bought, vacations taken – but everybody knows it can all end in an instant.

For our family, the big one came in 1993, my last year of high school. As usual, I came home at 3 p.m. to find Dad, not at all as usual, sitting on the green shag carpet of our living room. He was leaning against a wall with a box next to him. The job he had enjoyed for twenty-eight years – in effect, a job for life – had ended hours earlier and with little warning. In 1987, a British company called Allied-Lyons had bought Hiram Walker and now, finally, corporate cost-cutting and downsizing had reached Dad's department. Middle-aged employees like him were replaced by younger ones with smaller salaries and less vacation time. These cuts were received somewhat differently than the regular layoff threats my unionized mom received at GM. There was no call-back or seniority mechanisms in these lower- to mid-level management jobs. You were done for good. Dad had been told to pack up his personal things and was escorted out of the office by people he had socialized with for years. When I opened the door and saw him there, I knew exactly what was happening and, as distressing as this was, it was as if it were meant to be. This was the moment everyone in Windsor waits for, and now it was our turn.

One year later, a new casino opened in the city. A casino can be a kind of ironic economic stimulus machine that takes away as much as it gives to the communities in which it's located. But in post-NAFTA Windsor, with automotive jobs moving south, it brought with it – excuse the pun – a new jackpot of well-paying employment. Dad trained to be a blackjack dealer and was hired early on in the casino's temporary site in the former Art Gallery of Windsor's riverfront location. The expulsion of the gallery, a quintessentially middle-class place, in favour of working-class jobs, was an allegory for the city – a story about what, for many Windsorites, really matters. The gallery was moved temporarily to the mall, and while there was objection to the change, the surprising increase in attendance – to record levels, in fact – made the arrangement a case study in how to get people out to see art. The casino eventually moved to its permanent location a few blocks away, while the gallery got a fabulous new building. (It's now struggling financially, with the same low attendance it suffered from pre-casino, and a precarious position in the City's funding formula.)

Dad, for his part, settled into the casino for seven years. But burnt by the downsizing, he fell into line with Nana's views, arguing that a relatively safe union job where you punch in and out every day was preferable to the risks of a white-collar career. It was not a complete departure from his earlier thinking – even though he had occupied a somewhat adversarial managerial role at Hiram Walker, he always maintained that whatever employee gains the union made, white-collar workers received the same soon after. It was the Windsor system; people knew how it worked. Or some of them did, anyway. At the casino, Dad found that because they had hired so many people, there were many employees who had never worked in a union environment before. As a result, solidarity across job categories – 'card dealer' and 'security,' say – was hard to come by, even though all employees shared a union, the CAW. The effect was, unlike at the auto plants, a loss of cohesion.

Working-class Windsor is forever under economic and bureaucratic threat just as California is constantly under the threat of natural forces – not just earthquakes, but drought, the Santa Ana winds, wildfire. Joan Didion writes about this acutely in 'Los Angeles Notebook':

> It is hard for people who have not lived in Los Angeles to realize how radically the Santa Ana figures into the local imagination. The city burning is Los Angeles's deepest image of itself; Nathanael West perceived that, in *The Day of the Locust*; and at the time of the 1965 Watts riots what struck the imagination most indelibly were the fires. For days one could drive the Harbor Freeway and see the city on fire, just as we had always known it would be in the end. Los Angeles weather is the weather of catastrophe, of apocalypse, and, just as the reliably long and bitter winters of New England determine the way life there, so the violence and the unpredictability of the Santa Ana affect the entire quality of life in Los Angeles, accentuate its impermanence, its unreliability. The wind shows us how close to the edge we are.

I always knew I'd eventually find one of my parents sitting on the living room floor, immobilized by despair.

And then I moved to a city where I was suddenly consorting with a large population of people who rarely know how close that edge is, though there are many Torontonians who struggle, living lives like many people in Windsor do and did, in a city that's even more expensive and hostile to those with precarious employment or limited income. Instead of worrying about it – instead of doing something about it – people were obsessing over brunch. If Nero were around today, he would have brunched as Rome burned. What is it about this class of people that keeps them from seeing the fire?

The Middle Class
to the Brunching Class

If being working-class is characterized by a keen awareness of the fragility of economic stability, what does being *middle-class* mean, and how does this so-called creative class subset fit in? Easily, it seems, because so much can be called middle-class. The phrase *middle-class* is one we hear so often and in so many situations that it's assumed everyone knows what that phrase means and that we all share in a similar definition of it, and that we're all members of that class. But that definition is something we avoid addressing precisely because we don't know – or perhaps don't really *like* – what that definition might be because many of us might be excluded by it and find we're in a class we thought we didn't belong to. Perhaps it's a bit of both – ignorance and distaste often go hand in hand. And like the very nature of work itself, the definition of middle-class has changed over time and varies depending on who is being asked to define it. When pressed, many people will reflexively refer to middle-class consumption, a vague assortment of lifestyle and consumer products or processes: piano lessons, hockey practice, museum outings, backyard pool parties, waiting around for a delivery truck that will bring a new couch. Marketers crave the middle class's money. The members of the middle class own things and they own the home those things belong in; at least, that's conventional aspirational wisdom. The home, in fact, occupies centre stage in the life of the middle class. It needs redecorating, renovating and reorganizing often. Think of how many advertisements and lifestyle magazine exhortations – for everything from cleaning products to how to plan the perfect garden party – appeal to the idea of home ownership and maintenance. We never see Mr. Clean's bald head and muscular arms in a bachelor apartment. He has enough on his plate with all those nuclear families and the dull floors of their detached homes.

Middle-class consumption is a complicated thing, but crucial to understanding how this class self-identifies. When I moved to Toronto in 2000, the economy was booming. I was only a recent grad student with little job experience, however, so I started temping at a call centre. A giant call centre is not unlike a factory floor, and for a little while, at least, Toronto felt a bit more like Windsor (in fact, one of the ways Windsor has replaced its manufacturing sector is with much lower-paying call centres, a shift from an industrial economy to a service-oriented one). After four months of searching, however, I finally got a proper, permanent job as a fundraising researcher at a large non-profit organization. Not only was I tasked with finding the kind of philanthropic money unfamiliar to me in Windsor, I found out quickly that the people I worked with often had backgrounds very different than mine. My direct co-worker was a middle-aged woman newly returned to the workforce. Her kids were nearly adults: one was away at university and the other went to a high school she referred to by the mysterious initials UCC. I simply nodded along until it became apparent that UCC signified something special, and after quietly looking it up, I discovered that the letters stood for Upper Canada College, a large private school that many members of the country's elite had attended. Apart from perhaps a foreign student or two in university, she was the first person I had met who had been to, or sent a kid to, a private school. I suddenly learned about high school degrees that weren't just regular degrees but 'International Baccalaureates.' They were important. Heretofore I hadn't thought of my own high school degree as anything other than a standard-issue, top-of-the-line public school degree equal to all others in North America. Now I wondered what I had missed out on; this baccalaureate sounded special. I later found out my boss also went to a private school in Toronto, and later still, I met more and more people with the same background. These were families who had also been getting post-secondary educations for generations.

As I spent time in Toronto, I became aware of how vast this demographic was, with entire neighbourhoods, shopping areas, restaurants and social venues supporting it. It was a city within a city. There was talk of cottages, attendance at symphonies and the opera, memberships at art galleries. These were all things that, while not precisely foreign, were not part of my personal experience previously; if a trip was planned for the museum, discount tickets were sought, not a more expensive membership, as the museum was a special trip, not a regularly reoccurring experience. My co-workers were not alien creatures; they became friends, just ones with very different backgrounds. I had to learn a cursory amount about the local theatre scene in order to keep up in some conversations. References were made to esteemed individuals I had never heard of, like notable local chefs or music conductors, or to shops that were landmark destinations in neighbourhoods the alternative weekly papers didn't write about. Other prominent figures, professors or distinguished leaders of institutions, people with Order of Canada honours (the Canadian equivalent of a knighthood), were referred to offhandedly, almost in a personal way that implied a familiarity with those who were powerful and tastemakers. Who was this unfamiliar cohort? It wasn't exactly the rich or ruling class per se, but rather the enormous swath of people who lay just underneath the super-elite, supporting it like an aspirational pyramid.

This class was bigger than I ever could have imagined (had it ever occurred to me to imagine it), and it had its own aspirations and affluence. One of its haunts, a large sporting goods and clothing retailer called Sporting Life, both embodied and served these people. The store possessed a preppy, Hamptons-like aura and sold snowboards and skis alongside Prada and Armani casual wear. On busy weekends, its flagship location often has an off-duty cop directing suvs and foreign-made cars into its parking lot. Nearby, a high-end supermarket called Pusateri's also had an off-duty cop directing the same cars in and out of its lot. This class of people existed in its own ecosystem, a far cry from the one-size-fits-all mall I knew and worked in back in Windsor. Though my new job paid less than the one I had seven years earlier at the distillery, I was nonetheless now crossing the threshold into this world.

While many people equate middle-class with middle-class consumption, discussions about exactly what constitutes the middle class rarely address income. Being or feeling middle-class is about much more than numerical data. It's a world view, a sensibility, a sense of self. But, curiously, it's a sense of self that cuts across incomes. In a 2006 World Values Survey, more than a thousand Americans were asked which income decile they thought they were part of, with each decile representing 10 percent of the population (that is, the highest decile contained the top 10 percent of the population's income earners, and each subsequent decile contained the next, lower, income group). The survey was designed to gauge perceptions of socio-economic standing rather than actual income. Fewer than 20 percent of respondents placed themselves in either the top thirty or bottom twenty percentiles, with the majority stating that their income positioned them toward or directly in the middle of the spread. Canadians were also asked outright what social class they fell into. Fifty-five percent of Americans saw themselves as upper-middle or lower-middle-class (with 30 percent working-class) while 64 percent of Canadians were spread evenly across the two middle-class categories (with a similar 30 percent working-class). Fewer than 10 percent of both Americans and Canadians placed themselves in either the upper or lower extremes.

'I think if you polled people and asked if they were lower-, middle- or upper-class you would probably get 80 to 85 percent of the population seeing themselves as middle-class,' says Mike Moffat, an economist at the Richard Ivey School of Business at the University of Western Ontario in London, Ontario. 'At that point, the definition is meaningless.' Moffat himself grew up in East London, in a blue-collar enclave in what is generally a white-collar town. He points out that what makes defining the middle class problematic is that many people who became wealthy – lawyers, doctors or successful business people – grew up in places like Windsor or East London, but are making money that pulls them well out of the middle class, and still tend to think of themselves based on where they came from, where their parents worked or where they went to school. Those same people, Moffat argues, retain the sensibilities of their youth, and when they return to their hometowns to visit friends and family, that sensibility is reinforced again and again. 'They can never escape it,' he says. It's like the Jennifer Lopez song, 'Jenny from the Block,' where she tells her fans, at the peak of her superstardom, she hasn't changed. It doesn't matter where she is now – she's always from the South Bronx. All our identities are prone to Jenny-from-the-Block Syndrome.

The idea that we're all middle-class holds particular appeal for politicians. In speeches, debates and television ads, they make it clear they care about the middle class: 'The middle class needs saving.' 'The middle class is at risk.' 'The foundations of the middle class are crumbling and need shoring up.' When not being warned of its imminent demise, the middle class will be reminded that they are the bedrock of society, the foundation upon which everything else rests; as the middle class goes, so goes everything and everyone else. Find a politician who doesn't identify somehow with the middle class and you will have an unelectable fringe candidate. In a 2013 speech about – what else? – middle-class prosperity, U.S. president Barack Obama referred to 'families who worked hard and believed in the American Dream, but felt that the odds were increasingly stacked against them. And they were right.' He went on say, 'In the period after World War II, a growing middle class was the engine of our prosperity. Whether you owned a company, swept its floors or worked anywhere in between, this country offered you a basic bargain – a sense that your hard work would be rewarded with fair wages and benefits, the chance to buy a home, to save for retirement and, above all, to hand down a better life for your kids.' Obama's definition of the middle class was extremely wide and inclusive, with little room on either end of the spectrum. Despite the vast differences between an unskilled labourer and a CEO, to Obama they were all members of the middle class. Similarly, in 2012, British prime minister David Cameron vowed to build an aspirational middle-class nation composed of those who 'want to be better off, those who strive to make a better life for themselves.' In Canada, a 2013 Liberal Party television ad for Justin Trudeau, leader of the party and currently looking to unseat Conservative prime minister Stephen Harper, depicts him saying, 'My priority is the Canadians who built this country. The middle class, not the political class.' He adds this caveat: 'My priority is an economy that benefits us all, not just a few. My priority is you.' Any Canadian, regardless of socio-economic class, would naturally assume Trudeau is speaking to them as they, too, are part of the middle class.

Sometimes politicians call this venerated class of people 'working families.' This sounds suspiciously like 'working class,' but it's really just another way of saying middle class. It's an appeal to the values and security of the majority that politician represents, with variations on a kind of ecumenical work-ethic theme in which busyness is next to godliness. The phrase will often be reduced simply to 'families,' and repeated ad infinitum, as if that word itself was holy and saying it over and over will evoke a moral weight that makes a position or policy platform untouchable. It's similar to the way some exhort others to 'think of the children,' in the hopes of enhancing any argument that can't stand on its own.

But, in fact, we are not all middle-class and this is a problem. On the economics blog *Worthwhile Canadian Initiative*, economist Frances Woolley suggests that people live 'in their own worlds,' characterizing a typical person's internal reasoning as, 'I'm not as well off as the people across the street with the slightly nicer car and slightly better job, but I'm slightly better off than the people down the road who seem to be struggling a bit financially, so I guess that puts me around the middle of the income distribution.' This kind of reasoning makes it possible to accept middle-class messages as personal ones, even if they don't quite fit. Woolley goes on to point out that this perception has public policy consequences. As fewer people identify with people who have lower incomes, those people become *other people*, and support for the social and economic programs designed for those people erodes. This explains, in part, why politicians constantly appeal to the middle class. Despite a culture that nominally celebrates individuality, most people are inclined to think of themselves as part of the pack, as 'normal' or 'average,' and certainly not *below* average. Middle-class has become synonymous with average. And in a perfunctorily egalitarian society, where there is a certain coyness around extreme wealth, few readily admit to being at the top of the pile (*Keeping Up with the Kardashians* notwithstanding). Politicians prefer to keep the definition of middle-class vague because it allows them the illusion that they're speaking to everybody at once. The cycle feeds itself: as more politicians and media types speak to a broad though amorphous middle class, more people naturally come to associate themselves with it, diminishing a sense of their true economic position and leading to an inability to relate to policies that might actually benefit them.

The strength of the fiction that we're all middle-class intensifies when income disparity is discussed. How can you have income disparity if everyone is seemingly part of the same broad class? Sensibility is so powerful it can maintain a middle-class identity even when the wages are working-class. Anna Bowness, a writer and editor I met when I first arrived in Toronto, has written about the middle-class sensibility and coined the phrase *glass bottom* to describe what she sees as its most distinctive characteristic. Anna also grew up in London, halfway between Windsor and Toronto, a city as white-collar as Windsor is blue, Mike Moffat's East London neighbourhood aside. She was raised in a home that had more books and literature than mine and in a family given to more high-culture endeavours, though financially speaking, during the good times anyway, my family was probably a little better off. Anna argues that the middle class has a glass bottom below which, or through which, they cannot fall (and that their world view always incorporates), no matter how difficult their financial hardship. 'In the middle class, there are pockets of money and other resources that only get discovered when they're needed,' she explains. 'You think you are broke, but then you discover an old savings bond, or a stash of money from an investment you forgot about, or a relative swoops in and gives you a little boost. Whereas in the working and welfare classes, those hidden resources aren't there. When you run out of money, you run out of money. In a middle-class scenario, there is always one more last resort.'

Her description conjures in my mind those old British and continental aristocrats whose hereditary wealth had dried up, leaving them to live like paupers in their drafty, decaying old manor homes. Or, closer to home, the Beales of *Grey Gardens* fame, Jackie O's cousin and aunt, seemingly oblivious to their Hampton mansion collapsing around them in the 1970s while they talk about Broadway shows. In conventional families, it's a sensibility that allows the middle class to go into debt so the kids can keep taking piano and ballet lessons, or spend valuable time waiting in line for brunch. It's about where value is placed, and the lengths to which people go to maintain those kinds of activities. When cracks form in the glass bottom, they're usually out of view.

Anna is a card-carrying member of the creative class (were there cards to carry and if she wanted to actually carry one), but both of us sidled into this class from different directions by making determined choices in our careers. Membership here is heterogeneous, as a certain amount of class mobility has allowed us to find our way into the careers we have. Yet the level of class-consciousness isn't equal (nor is mobility, for that matter). Coming from a working-class direction and moving upward affords a privileged view of class: the lower you go, the more there is to notice up top. In Anna's case, her own penchant for observing such things came about from her Scottish ancestors, who emigrated after the war, and being exposed to first-generation newcomers from the U.K. who talk about class in ways we in North America don't. While my nana wondered why I didn't go into a solid tool-and-die job, other members of the creative classes came from upper middle and upper classes, so their tension would be in moving downward, economically, of having to explain why they didn't follow their parents into law, medicine or finance, embarking instead on precarious careers with much lower wages and fewer benefits like pensions or medical coverage. It should be noted that these are not people slumming like those depicted in the great 1990s class anthem by Pulp, 'Common People,' but simply people who followed their dreams and ambitions as much as I did because they wanted to do something they liked doing. Children of immigrants may feel this most acutely, as their parents – first-generation newcomers – worked the hardest to make their way into the security and comfort the middle class seemingly provided, making many personal sacrifices along the way, only to see their children reject it by choosing a creative career. All shifts come with their own baggage, some more than others, and perspectives on class will differ depending on which direction an individual came from.

Self-perception can do a lot for confidence, but it can also lead people astray by obfuscating what's in the best interest of the individual, a phenomenon described by Thomas Frank in his 2004 book, *What's the Matter with Kansas? How Conservatives Won the Heart of America*. Frank wrote of how a history of entrenched traditional left-wing populism in his home state disappeared as Kansas became a deeply conservative state, voting overwhelmingly Republican even as the party supported policies that went against the best economic interests of most Kansans. Part of the power of conservative populism is the ability to seem anti-elite while maintaining an elite status quo by appealing to lifestyle and cultural wedge issues like abortion and gay marriage, two of the examples Frank uses in his book, that supersede economic issues. Values are what count and what people identify with. It happened in Kansas, but it's happened in places as diverse as Toronto, where our disgraced crack-smoking mayor, Rob Ford, came into power with the support of vast numbers of working-class people who would have been ultimately affected by the cuts he threatened to city services, and in Macomb County, the suburban Detroit collection of bedroom communities where a similar set of forces was behind the 'Reagan Democrat' phenomenon in the 1980 and 1984 U.S. federal elections. Here traditionally Democratic voters swung right in landslide numbers, voting for Republican Ronald Reagan in both elections. It didn't matter to the many Macomb County residents who worked in the auto plants that Reagan struck a massive body blow against the labour movement when he fired air traffic controllers in 1981. He continued to find appeal in folksy rhetoric and calls for a return to traditional values, the kind Archie and Edith Bunker sang about in the opening of the 1970s television sitcom *All In the Family*. When values are involved, it's easy for anyone to slip into false perceptions that undermine their own well-being.

Contemporary Western life is largely defined by how we fill it with work and leisure. Everybody has to work. Some of us are lucky enough to choose what we do with our work, a luxury often as much dependent on where and to whom you were born as on the choices you make. There's also personal work to keep individuals and families chugging along: child care, laundry, grocery shopping, household repairs – the usual domestic to-do list. This alone is an essential full-time job for many.

Then there's free time. What people do with their free time is golden, a cherished interregnum that most use how they please and that is increasingly endangered. In 2010, the Canadian Index of Wellbeing at the University of Waterloo released a report called 'Caught in the Time Crunch: Time Use, Leisure and Culture in Canada.' Its findings were not surprising. For one thing, it reported that Canadians 'perceive and spend time much differently than they once did,' and that leisure and cultural activities were changing as a result. Urban sprawl and longer commutes had shrunk free time while laptops and smartphones created a workforce that was perpetually on call. Longer working hours, providing care to an aging population and working non-standard shifts have also devoured more time and reduced leisure. Further, time constraints were worse for people 'marginalized by race, ethnicity, religion, socioeconomic status, dis/ability, gender, sexual orientation and language proficiency, [and who] experience systemic barriers to social and economic opportunity.' Though the report argued that leisure 'contributes to the wellbeing of individuals, communities, and societies,' it found that the average portion of total time that Canadians spent on leisure and social activities went from 15 percent in 1998 to 12 percent in 2005, with the largest drop experienced by women. The study concluded, in part, that while a decline in leisure bodes poorly for individual wellbeing, these activities 'also help shape our national identity and sense of who we are as a people.' So how we spend our free time matters, and with less of it to go around, the choices we make are more important than ever – and many are choosing to brunch.

We don't need the University of Waterloo to tell us that leisure time is in short supply. Is there anyone, save the retirees, who would admit to being less busy, less put upon and less a target of demanding obligations now than they were before? We are the busiest generation ever. Not being busy means there's a problem:

illness, a recession, personal sloth. We're as busy as the stylists that Morrissey famously sang about on his 1988 B-side 'Hairdresser on Fire.' Ever the astute chronicler of the working and middle classes, Morrissey dipped his pallid finger into the flow of late-Thatcher modern British life and saw which way and how fast it was going. 'And you're always busy,' Morrissey sang about London during the high-cash-flow flash and bang of the 1980s, but he could have been crooning about any large city in the Western world today, whose denizens are equally occupied, packing their days with work and tasks and, most importantly, keeping up a proper appearance while doing it.

Little has changed in the twenty-five years since Morrissey recorded the tune, though the arrival of the Internet has certainly accelerated things even further – we can now, potentially, be busy twenty-four hours a day. With ever more precarious and provisional employment, the disappearance of the conventional eight-hour workday and the consequent contraction of leisure time, examining how exactly the contemporary, urban middle class spends its free time can explain who exactly the middle class is and how it understands itself. How we spend time is also about how we allocate value in conditions where time is often not in our complete control, making it even more precious.

When I return to Windsor, time seems different, slower, but that's based on my memory of the highly structured working life of so many people in a handful of large industrials with very regular hours. Even into the 1980s, when they were already in decline, manufacturing-based economies in the developed world insisted on a certain amount of broad, regimented routine. People woke and went either to the office, shop or factory for the workday and then filled the hours between work and sleep with tasks or leisure activities. Except for the executive or professional who brought work home on evenings and weekends, the forty-hour workweek was largely sacrosanct. They seemed like exceptions, however, high-functioning outliers who chose careers outside the established norms of modern middle-class society.

Now these outliers have become the norm. Our working lives today spill far beyond the traditional forty hours. If your life still adheres to the schedule established during the industrial age, you probably work in a unionized environment, or for the government. When I had a proper nine-to-five office job, I arrived at work, possibly stopping to get coffee first, settled into my seat and switched my desktop computer on, waited for it to boot up, then opened email. There usually wasn't much that I hadn't already seen because most of the people I interacted with also worked nine-to-five, and as only a few people had BlackBerry smartphones at the time, little work occurred outside those hours. Now if I open my laptop after fifteen or sixteen hours of not checking email, I would be filled with anxiety, knowing there are emails waiting for me, some of them that needed tending to hours ago and some from people I work with in other time zones, on other continents. That would never happen, though, because even if I didn't open my computer, I'd have already seen the emails on my iPhone or iPad, which are always on and routinely checked. Even when I don't need or want to answer an email, the only way to keep anxiety at bay is to know what emails have come in.

People who advocate turning everything off for a weekend, going camping where there is no wifi or cellular signal, as a way to relax, describe what must be the most torturous days of being in the dark, of not knowing if something is falling apart, or needs doing, or if they're about to lose one of their jobs because they're not on top of it. Multifaceted creative careers are like spinning plates that need to be constantly maintained. It's unrelenting. So, like many people, I check email as I wake up in the morning, lying in bed still half asleep with the phone in my hand, both propped up on a pillow so I don't have to lift my head to see the screen. Often I'm shocked awake in a panic by something I read; it's much more efficient than hitting the snooze button. There are also Facebook and Twitter responses to check, some of which are work, some not, some both.

In France, the epidemic of always being on, whether paid or not, was addressed recently when a new deal with employees in the technology and consultancy sectors required them to clock out for a set amount of time to rest, with penalties to employers if they breached this by expecting them to, say, answer emails promptly, when they were ostensibly off. Yet, how do they resist? Our devices are our burden, yet we suffocate without them. We take them everywhere, even into the bathroom. I've seen so many men standing at a urinal, one hand down below, the other fingering his BlackBerry, scrolling through messages while holding the two most important things in his life. Phones must be the filthiest devices we touch, carried into and out of toilets without even a Purell rubdown. Should a cholera epidemic ever break out, look to the phones first.

Offices today, which in cities are sometimes located in refurbished buildings that were once warehouses or manufacturing plants, often look more like cafés or artists' lofts than the grids of desks familiar from *Mad Men*. Like many brunch venues, workplace decor often alludes back to rougher occupations, where swank loft offices still have traces of the garment factory that once existed there, preserved because it's cool, just like places of leisure such as cafés and restaurants in refurbished factory spaces that keep some references to the old dirty work that occurred here, suggesting everybody's just on a coffee break, waiting for the back-to-work whistle to blow. As the line between work and leisure blurs, so too does the divide between personal and professional. In the past, the boss and employees could be social, some were often friends, but the hierarchy was always there. Today it's all mixed up, like an old-fashioned company picnic but with no rules. As a writer you might work for an editor who in turn writes for you on another project. I've had friends who had to fire friends from long-term writing gigs, then had to hang around together at mutual friend's house party soon after. Some friendships are destroyed, but often it's just sucked up, and organic friendships come under stress when one friend controls the destiny of another, financially or otherwise. What happens if you owe somebody overdue work, but you're overworked and need to blow off some steam with friends, but the person you owe the work to is out with your friends? That's when you drink alone at home.

The lack of clear hierarchy also means money issues can get weird, especially when a friend asks you to work on a project with low pay but a lot of social or cultural good. There's a sense of obligation to help a friend out, and so often the money is not discussed. *You're an artist – could you just fire off an illustration for me? Tiny budget, sorry. Hey, writer, this project I'm working on is really great – could you make a blog post about it to give it some oxygen?* Saying no to these kinds of work requests can make you feel like a jerk. And the money? Why would friends have to discuss such gauche details? But resentments fester because things go unpaid or underpaid, and are rarely talked about in order to preserve social decorum. The strange part is, because there's no hierarchy, and creative economies run in multiple directions, the victims are also the victimizers, and we keep doing it to each other. We need to start talking about this to figure out a way to install some kind of order or system – a true hierarchy might be antithetical in a truly egalitarian creative economy – that prevents us from giving away our time and work so easily.

The notion of a middle class that incorporated leisure into its identity was first coined as such by Thorstein Veblen, a curious sociologist and economist who put out his most well-known work, *The Theory of the Leisure Class*, in 1899. Taking nearly a decade of his life to produce, Veblen's critique of social and economic behaviour describes the evolution of what he called 'conspicuous leisure' and 'conspicuous consumption,' two behaviours that had permeated modern life as he saw it. Large parts of his theory are also uncanny descriptions of contemporary brunch scenes and its participants, but his book has remained just on the outside of mainstream thought.

Veblen's mercurial life took him from the Wisconsin frontier to completing a PhD in philosophy at Yale and teaching gigs at Harvard, University of Chicago and Stanford, where his chaotic personal life often led to his being fired for adultery. As sad as his life was, Veblen managed to write a dense book that was not without wit. In it, he describes not just the leisure class of his time, but also how today's brunching class came to be and how a leisure activity could become so much a part of one's identity.

Taking an evolutionary view of economics and society, he suggests the leisure class began in the higher stages of barbarian culture, or feudal times, when a distinction was made between various classifications of employment between the classes; suddenly there was a difference between grunt work and intellectual and artisanal work. 'Manual labour, industry, whatever has to do directly with the everyday work of getting a livelihood, is the exclusive occupation of the inferior class,' he wrote. With some exceptions, including the manufacture and care of arms and the handling of horses, dogs, and hawks, manual labour by higher classes was frowned upon. Exceptions today might still include working with horses, a hobby for some in the middle class; walking the fancy dogs at the Westminster Dog Show in New York City; or perhaps trades such as furniture making or other practices of high design, where craft is elevated above mere labour. Running a tool-and-die shop in Windsor probably doesn't cut it.

Instead of work, then, leisure became a dominant part of identity. 'The institution of a leisure class,' Veblen writes, 'is the outgrowth of an early discrimination between employments, according to which some employments are worthy and others unworthy.' People made these distinctions between 'exploit and drudgery,' what today might be called manufacturing and the higher order, intellectual work that affords time to enjoy leisure activities. This class spent a considerable amount of time acquiring and demonstrating a knowledge of decorum, of knowing what to do and when to do it, 'what is known as manners and breeding,' writes Veblen, the things that are 'imperatively insisted on.' These refined tastes, manners and habits of life are the 'useful evidence of gentility, because good breeding requires time, application, and expense, and can therefore not be compassed by those whose time and energy are taken up with work.' And the more time all this takes up, the greater the esteem. Often, as I found in my shift into the middle class, not knowing even the subtlest kinds of decorum, even the things that are so easy to fake by watching other people or looking it up quickly, like knowing the difference between Merlot and Malbec, is just enough to nudge one's balance off during a social event.

Veblen charts the emergence of this new leisure class coinciding with ownership and what the owning of items means, something he calls 'pecuniary emulation,' that results in a need for 'trophies' that show off one's status. In barbarian times, this meant women or valuable objects; those 'trophies' evolved into the possession of wealth being the ultimate trophy and a meritorious act in itself. But a sense of chronic dissatisfaction would set in, as standards were always rising, fashion changing, and there was more wealth or a new trophy to chase. Veblen recognized that by modern times, leisure – in particular, conspicuous leisure and the ability to abstain from work – had become a trophy recognized 'by thoughtful men as a prerequisite to a worthy or beautiful, or even blameless, human life.' Veblen's definition of leisure is the non-productive consumption of time, an active notion rather than passive endeavour. Leisure doesn't just happen, it is pursued, then as now.

Now, however, the line between work and leisure is blurred for many in the middle class, as both have become so mixed up in our personal identity creation that sometimes we're writers but other times we're mountain bikers. The places we work have become more leisure-like too. When Google unveiled plans for its new London digs (scheduled to open in 2016), the *Telegraph* heralded its 'quirky take on the traditional office,' with Union Jack–emblazoned walls and surreal workspaces with names like the Velourmptious Snug, a green, padded homage to the British pub. The article quotes Lee Penson, the founder of the interior design and architecture firm responsible for the office, who describes it in decidedly non-corporate terms: 'It's all about human beings and that's it. Think sunken snugs, comfort, fun, comfy slippers, squishy carpets, cushions, daybeds, nice fresh food, gardening, vegetables, health, visual stimulation, relaxation, exercise, fresh air and you'll get what it's all about as an HQ.' Anyone who remembers the first dot-com bubble of the late 1990s is familiar with this kind of workspace. And though that bubble burst in the early 2000s, the aesthetic it spawned – which disguises work as play – remains popular. Does it make it easier to give up our leisure time when a meeting room is called a granny flat and designed in floral prints with easy chairs? What happens when work is going badly and a workspace that looks leisurely is suddenly a place of great stress? There is a cognitive dissonance in form and function here, perhaps the reason an event like brunch becomes such an overt act of leisure, even if in practice it isn't leisurely.

Many other people don't have anything resembling a workspace at all. Work happens everywhere now. Many of us work from home, or from actual cafés, freelance vagabonds who move from one rickety table to the next, renting the space with our coffee purchases, getting more wired as the day goes on. In January 2014, the *Guardian* reported that the first British branch of the Russian chain Ziferblat opened in Islington, a London neighbourhood well-known for its clusters of peripatetic knowledge workers. What makes Ziferblat (*clock face* in Russian) different is that it charges five pence per minute, and patrons get free snacks and coffee, and can make their own food in the kitchen. It's essentially like renting an office on a micro, minute-by-minute basis.

As permanent employment has slowly evaporated in favour of temporary and contract labour, many of us find ourselves with multiple jobs, sometimes spread over several different fields. Pivoting from one to another requires a remarkable amount of skill – the shifting of mental gears takes time. In turn, what used to be considered almost sacred free time has become instead a reservoir of potential work time that is drawn from all too frequently. Some people try to confront this phenomenon by organizing – in the labour union sense. There are unpaid interns and freelance writers worried about a work-life/work-pay/work-stability balance who join unions that haven't really worked yet in part because it's difficult to collectively represent people with extremely individualized working and earning habits with multiple clients. And who has the time to organize? Remember how busy everybody says they are? If such a state wasn't so readily accepted as our collective identity, we might stop talking about it and do something meaningful to change it.

This creative-class socio-economic subset of the middle class was identified and brought into popular thought by the academic

Richard Florida in his 2002 book *The Rise of the Creative Class*. Published just over one hundred years after Veblen published *Theory of the Leisure Class*, Florida's book came at a time when modern Western society had undergone major shifts since Veblen's era with deindustrialization and the emergence of a service-based economy. The commonality of the creative class is creative work, with human creativity being the 'ultimate economic resource,' according to Florida, and one that has a broad spectrum of people toiling away in professions and vocations that include scientists, engineers, artists, musicians, designers and knowledge-based professionals. Florida points out that in 1900, fewer than 10 percent of American workers were doing creative work, but by 2000 they represented a third of the workforce, with numbers between 25 percent and 30 percent in advanced European economies, but they had not been grouped together as such. 'This book describes the emergence of a new social class,' writes Florida in his preface, which reads as call to arms (or rather, pens, paintbrushes and guitars). 'If you are a scientist or engineer, an architect or designer, a writer, artist or musician, or if you use your creativity as a key factor in your work in business, education, health care, law or some other profession, you're a member.' The trouble was, and is, many of these people do not see their work as creative, and there is no natural unifying force around these kinds of workers. Florida was perplexed that, while he was chron-icling so much evidence of it, the creative class was largely unaware of its own existence. Unlike other classes that emerged in times of upheaval with strong senses of identity, they could not organize to improve their lot. To that end, he called on the creative class to 'grow up' and take control of its own destiny – essentially, form a class-consciousness.

As Florida's role as a public intellectual grew throughout the 2000s, he continued to push the creative-class notion and travel to cities around the world, but in particular found an attentive audience in rust-belt cities and other economically depressed centres, places similar to Windsor, Detroit or Pittsburgh, the latter where he was a professor at Carnegie Mellon. Florida's message resonated in cities large and small that had seen their economic foundations collapse but that had untapped creative capacity in their un- and under-employed population, which, if unleashed, could be their salvation. These were, after all, cities where people knew how to make actual things. There were critics, though. The risk a public intellectual takes is allowing her message to get watered down and communicated broadly in sound-bite chunks that miss some of the conceptual and evidence-based underpinnings, perhaps at no fault of their own, and Florida was sometimes called a carpetbagger or huckster, selling ideas in desperate places.

In 2007 he left Pittsburgh for a high-profile job heading up the Martin Prosperity Institute at the University of Toronto's Rotman School of Management. Already a star in academic and urban circles, Florida's arrival in Toronto was met with typical Canadian enthusiasm when an American of note pays attention to us, and he was feted and given ample coverage. The *Globe and Mail* newspaper even awarded him a monthly column called 'Richard Florida Visits,' where he offered an outsider's first impressions of Toronto, awkwardly packaged with a strong whiff of Canadian desperation (akin to Sally Field's 'You like me, right now, you like me' Oscar speech) that set Florida up for some blowback, particularly from the would-be creative class itself. A group of critical artists and writers in Toronto even started a group called Creative Class Struggle, which did not hide their antipathy to Florida and his large salary at a public university, but they also engaged in activism examining who gets left out of the much-touted 'creative city' and who gets to participate, all of which are worthy and necessary investigations.

What is most curious about the wider, negative reaction, a lot of which I watched as it passed through my social media network in the form of snark directed at Florida and the idea of a creative class, is that his book itself is very much a numbers-driven, evidence-based call to critically rethink our working lives and our leisure time. He encourages us to consider how the balance might be off, and, most importantly, how this new class hasn't a class consciousness in the same way traditional working-class populations did. This last point is key, and may be precisely why the creative class has met considerable resistance among progressives and those whose ideas about work and identity are more ideological.

In his chapter titled 'The Transformation of Everyday Life,' Florida writes, 'In this new world, it is no longer the organizations we work for, churches, neighbourhoods or even family ties that define us. Instead, we do this ourselves, defining our identities along the varied dimensions of our creativity. Other aspects of our lives – what we consume, new forms of leisure and recreation, efforts at community-building – then organize themselves around this process of identity creation.' Florida goes on to loosen the connection between income and class, just as Moffat and others do, but he goes further, suggesting that a '*class* is a cluster of people who have common interests and tend to think, feel and behave similarly, but these similarities are fundamentally determined by economic function – by the kind of work they do for a living. All the other distinctions follow from that.' When compared to old forms of labour organizing around class, like what happened in Windsor in 1945 and the ninety-nine-day Ford strike that led to the Rand Formula that codified the rules around the unionization process, the creative class do not all work in the same place, for one employer or in one industry, so the connection to other co-workers and other kinds of work is not immediate, conceptually or geographically.

The creative class's prime economic function, according to Florida, is to create new ideas, new technology and/or new creative content – some 38 million Americans in total are engaged in these kinds of pursuits. The service class is sometimes lumped into the creative economy, but Florida says the distinction between those in the service sector and those in the creative class is autonomy in the latter; they are paid to create while the service class is paid to execute an already-created plan. It is curious why we do not speak more of the service class as the working class. Though not as physical as working in the Ford foundry, the punch-in/punch-out life is much the same, as is the lack of agency. Having worked in both sectors, from the factory floor at Hiram Walker to the mall record store (and even my first Toronto job temping at a call centre), I see much in common with the relationship to work (being told what to do) and a wider class sensibility (feeling as if somebody else controls your destiny).

As for lifestyle, Florida argues the creative class is not just a blending of bourgeois and bohemian values, as outlined in David Brook's 2000 book *Bobos in Paradise: The New Upper Class and How They Got There*, an early look at what would inform Florida's creative class, but transcends those two categories completely. 'Spurred on by the creative ethos, we blend work and lifestyle to construct our identities as creative people,' writes Florida. 'Today, the people in my interviews identify themselves through a tangle of connections to a myriad creative activities. One person may be simultaneously a writer, researcher, consultant, cyclist, rock climber, electronic/world music/acid jazz lover, amateur gourmet cook, wine enthusiast or micro-brewer.' Here Veblen and Florida meet as identity is formed as much by leisure pursuits as by work, but with so many variables and combinations, finding common ground between everyone is difficult. Florida even says it's almost impossible to be a non-conformist today because there is nothing to conform to. This lack of tangible establishment makes it difficult to find something to organize around, whether for or against.

Creative-class types tend to reject collectivist notions because such a high value is placed on individuality. Each person, as a creative producer, is unique, allowing her to create unique work. We are all auteurs. There's a ferocious clinging to the identity of non-conformity; nobody sneers at those automatons stuck in their office cubicles more than creatives, a sentiment illustrated in the 1999 film *Fight Club*, where the conformist suckers all have the same office furniture, the same Ikea condo decor, the same ideas and so on. The paradox, of course, is there's an intense conformity in being non-conformist. Working-class identities are much more comfortable being part of a collective because that's where power and agency historically come from.

At the risk of making too broad a generalization – especially toward younger Millennials – the self-esteem generations, where everyone was a special flower, may have contributed to the non-conformity, but there's an inherent entrepreneurial drive behind the creative class that necessitates some individuality. Freelancers and other creative producers are essentially small businesses that either work independently or partner with other organizations. In this way, they're more like traditional business people – they're even taxed as such; in Canada freelancers are classified as 'sole proprietors' of their personal business – so there's a similar approach to both income and where work and opportunity come from that, by necessity, is business-minded (rejecting this approach is one reason many talented artists have failed to make a go of their careers).

Yet with all this formal and informal encouragement of individuality, nobody eats brunch alone. Leisure activities are more often than not social ones; they are a shared experience, even if a niche pursuit. With a little more self-examination and class awareness, there's got to be enough room to maintain one's individuality – wherever that flag has been planted and creative personal space has been carved out – yet still recognize a common cause across the varied pursuits.

'My definition of class emphasizes the way people organize themselves into social groupings and common identities based principally on their economic function,' writes Florida, in a passage that gets to the heart of his new class. 'Their social and cultural preferences, consumption, and buying habits, and their social identities all flow from this.' Florida compares a creative people's ownership of property to Marx's notion of the working class, in that most do not own or control any significant property of their own 'in the physical sense,' but rather their property is in their heads, their creative capacity or, as Marx might put it, the work they can do. Florida argues that though they don't see themselves as a unique social grouping, creative people share enough similar tastes, desires and preferences that class coherence is emerging, though not one as distinct as the industrial working class. Some of the shared values Florida goes on to list include individuality, meritocracy, diversity and openness.

On the face of it, these seem like exactly the kinds of values a just and fair class identity should be based on and are in line with the principles expressed by most existing progressive organizations and people. However, in a section of his book called 'Post-Scarcity

Effect,' Florida looked at the work of Ronald Inglehard, a political science professor at University of Michigan who conducted his own world-values survey that found there was 'a worldwide shift from economic growth issues to lifestyle values, which [Inglehard] sometimes refers to as a shift from "survival" to "self-expression" values.' This can happen in industrial work too. Thinking back to the collective world view I shared with my fellow Windsorites, survival was always part of our identity – when would the 'big one' happen and what would we do? – but because the level of comfort the high-paying, unionized job provided, lifestyle values did become a part of our identity too, though I would argue not overwhelmingly so, as the identity around the industrial work itself remained dominant. Recall how difficult it was for my new friend at the Christmas party to even think of herself as a photographer rather than a line worker at Ford.

However, it's the creative class's penchant to identify with lifestyle issues rather than work that is most at odds with how class is traditionally identified by organized labour and left-leaning progressives. In this passage by Florida, based on a 2000 book called *The Cultural Creatives: How 50 Million People Are Changing the World* by sociologist Paul H. Ray and psychologist Sherry Ruth Anderson, he writes: 'Members of this group are more likely than others to be interested in personal development and relationships, have eclectic tastes, enjoy "foreign and exotic" experiences, and identify themselves as being "not financially materialistic." In short these cultural creatives are what Inglehart refers to as "post-materialist."'

This is the rub. If the creative class is truly postmaterialist, it becomes much harder for it to be identified and organized around old theories and ideologies, paradigms that have made sense since the industrial revolution kicked in and Marx wrote his famous book. Work seems like leisure, and leisure is work now; fewer people work at the same office, eat in the same cafeteria or complain around the same water cooler about the company that employs them. And yet everybody's brunching. The creative class could, and perhaps should, be called the 'brunching class.' Referring to this group of people as such would recognize that brunch and other similar leisure and lifestyle pursuits have become the common denominator among middle-class people working in a variety of knowledge-based fields. If a politicized identity and class consciousness could be formed around a pastime that is purely leisure, rather than through the work itself, a kind of rear attack on the problem could take place.

There are those who might resist the idea that the work they do is the kind of work that could create a class consciousness. Many who have never lived in a union or labour-movement environment may be unable to recognize a common cause like this; recall the newly minted casino workers my dad came in contact with who had never worked in a union environment and were resistant to notions of solidarity across job classification. Yet if we take a hard look at what many in the creative class do, there's potential if we start defining it in more simple terms. A moment early in my Toronto life suggests that the old idea of what labour is and Florida's new creative class can be reconciled, though the language is different and the work itself doesn't look like work used to. In searching for my first job, I had a handful of people I relied on to supply references when requested. Since I was a new graduate, it was a mix of an old part-time-job employer, my academic supervisor and a friend. That friend had gone on from grad school to a leadership position in a part of the Canadian student movement that remains stalwartly left-wing, with strong ties to the labour movement such that the students will sometimes sing the union anthem 'Solidarity Forever' at their meetings.

In the interview for the job that I ultimately got, my would-be boss told me he was impressed my friend had said I was 'suited well for intellectual labour' in his reference letter. It was the first time I had heard the phrase *intellectual labour*, and it hasn't come up often since, but it stuck with me because it changed the way I viewed what I did in school and what I hoped to do with the rest of my life, and moreover it directly connected with what I had done before in the record shop and in the factory too. It was all labour, only some was physical and some was not. Work is work. Isn't that what the creative class is – intellectual labour that takes place inside of Veblen's dynamic, interrelated web of lifestyle choices? However, instead of something that could create a shared sense of common cause or, dare I say, solidarity, we're left with brunch as it's often practiced: a religion of aesthetic wastefulness and little else.

The trouble with brunch is that it could be so much more, and a closer look at brunch itself reveals its potential. The brunching class, if it embraced a little Veblen and Florida, and took a critical look at how it spends its time, and how others around it do, a collective identity across heretofore loosely related kinds of knowledge workers could be formed. What's more, that the brunching class exists in places with radically different economic circumstances demonstrates it's a class consciousness that could be global in scope.

The Transnational Buenos Aires Brunch

It was nearly two o'clock on a Sunday afternoon and we were walking the near-deserted streets of Buenos Aires looking for a very particular brunch spot. In town for two weeks to attend an art symposium, I had made a new conference friend, Kate, also from Toronto and keen to find a place she had read about in her *Wallpaper City Guide: Buenos Aires*, an object she was a little sheepish about but one that was compact and listed just enough galleries and eating spots to suggest a few distractions for the spare hours during the busy week. 'Do you want to go to brunch tomorrow?' she had asked on Saturday night.

It's a question I dread, one that comes around often, usually offered with the best of intentions and met with what must seem like, at worst, rude indifference. I have a 'no brunch ever' rule that is as ironclad as it can be without turning me into a complete social pariah. At home, in Toronto, I just won't go, as there are plenty of other ways to socialize with friends and, to be frank, expressing a public disdain for this meal means rarely being invited anyway. There are exceptions to the rule. If the brunch is being held at a friend's home, that's different. That's more like a special visit or a dinner party, and dinner parties are okay because it's dinner, a normal meal with proper rules. As well, when travelling I will usually acquiesce to an invitation, especially if it's extended by the people I'm visiting who are excited to show me their city. For many, brunch is part of that tourist experience. If it's relatively quick, it can be useful and fuel for doing other things, but I find it difficult to hide my impatience if it stretches on. When I'm in another city, I want to *see* that city, not a brunch place that is likely a facsimile of the brunch places I don't frequent at home. Globalization has meant we can tour the world, go to the farthest corners, yet still get a Subway sandwich or a Starbucks Grande Soy Chai Latte, or find a leisure experience like brunch that recreates itself independently, without the corporate head office's guiding hand. All of that, and stopping for a meal as languid as brunch, can feel like a conspicuous waste of an expensive plane ticket; there's a city to explore.

There are two near-universal places I like to wander into when travelling: bars and malls. Other places tourists visit, such as museums or galleries, tend to be culturally programmed on specific subjects through either artifacts or art, or through the cuisine itself at restaurants. Generic bars, be they sports bars, dance bars, lounge bars or gay bars, tend to be more the same than different, as are malls. There's an archetype and it's followed. The rules are all laid out, but there are differences, usually subtle, that are interesting articulations of local culture. Part of these visits is an overt, if sometimes masochistic, tour of globalized culture, of seeing the sameness everywhere. It's a bit like people who go to Las Vegas because they can experience a simulation of Paris, New York, Venice and ancient Rome all in one city. Going to the mall is like seeing a bit of home somewhere far away, familiar and unfamiliar at the same time. It's interesting to see what the local mall chains in a given place are like; a mall in Colombia had a Juan Valdez coffee shop, and in Malta the malls have a preponderance of British and Italian chains rather than American, themselves British and Italian versions of various American brands. Mostly it's a great place to people-watch in conditions that are like a base or constant in chemistry, something similar everywhere that local culture can bounce off of. Bars, where people tend to let loose, are fine places to see how people mix and interact informally. Do people dance to music, or do they stand around, reluctant to move? Taking note of what's different in all the sameness is important, but so too is seeing what's the same. And there's a lot that repeats in widely disparate places. Brunch, it turns out, is as globalized as the Gap. So, despite my usual feelings, going to brunch in Buenos Aires seemed more compelling than it does back home or in a more familiar city.

'Brunch?' I asked. Kate smiled enthusiastically, and, as I often do, I immediately felt bad for thinking of ways to say no, so I said yes. Most, if not all, brunch invitations are extended with only goodwill, so declining, or even thinking of declining, comes with its share of guilt. Anyway, this was brunch in Buenos Aires, which made it worthwhile for a few reasons. A long walk with a new friend to a new neighbourhood in a new city is good enough reason alone, and since city exploration for me is mostly a solo endeavour by circumstance, doing it with somebody else is a nice change. But this was also Argentina, an entire hemisphere away from Toronto and a country with a different history and culture, and most importantly, a recent economic crisis where people lost their entire life savings overnight and hundreds of thousands of citizens marched the streets in 'pots-and-pans' protests, a rare moment of class consciousness among the middle class. Surely brunch had to be different here.

The crisis, known sometimes as the Argentine Great Depression, reached its zenith in late 2001, when protests had turned to riots, leaving several people dead on the streets of Buenos Aires, a city built in a glorious colonial style that suggests deep wealth and stability. Yet Argentina has experienced more than its share of dramatic recent history during the Peronist era, which included Evita's cult of personality, and during the military dictatorship, which ruled between 1976 and 1983, carrying out a campaign of state terrorism called the Dirty War that saw the persecution of liberal and leftist middle- and working-class populations, including the disappearance or murder of an estimated 20,000 people. It also led the country into the demoralizing Falklands War defeat in 1982. All of this remains in the living memory of many Argentineans today, as does the crisis a decade ago for those too young to remember the earlier national traumas, an event the country is still slowly recovering from.

With the *Wallpaper* guide in hand, we left Recoleta, the downtown neighbourhood our hotel was in, and started out on the hour-long walk to the Palermo Soho neighbourhood, touted in the guide and elsewhere as the trendiest, most fashionable and chic part of the city – Buenos Aires' answer to Williamsburg or Prenzlauer Berg. Buenos Aires likes to take Sunday off, so there wasn't much happening as we walked the low-rise commercial and residential streets of Palermo, the artisan shops and unique boutiques listed in the guide closed for the day. Though we began to wonder if we were lost, this is what I had hoped for – a city unfolding in front of us as we wandered. In anticipation of brunch, we hadn't eaten breakfast, so our hunger was growing. But because this was an 'emerging' neighbourhood, as trendy ones often are, there weren't even any old-school corner cafés or bars that we might have ducked into like we could have in a more commercially established part of town.

The place we were looking for was called Oui Oui, a decidedly brunchy kind of name, and, as we turned a corner in the vicinity of where we thought it should be, we knew we had found our destination. Even a block away it was obvious because it was the only place with a group of people waiting outside, and nothing says a *Wallpaper*-approved brunch like a loitering crowd. As we approached along a narrow, cobblestoned street lined with tall plane trees, the dozen or so people standing on the sidewalk came into sharper view. It was as if a casting director had instructed a group of well-dressed extras with elaborately tied scarves to stand in a line that didn't look like a line. Non-conformists, all of them, like their non-conformist cousins in Toronto and elsewhere. Directly in front of the small restaurant itself was a row of five or six pink wooden patio tables and chairs with a handful of people sitting down at them, arms folded to ward off the cool May air. In the middle of each table, as at so many brunch places around the world, a Mason jar had been repurposed to hold cut roses.

We made our way past this human tableau to the front door and did the apprehensive 'We're-not-cutting-we're-just-checking' door opening where we were met by a fashionable and frowning hostess who sighed and, looking at the non-line, said, in English, it would be a while before something inside was available, but we could sit outside immediately if we wanted to, so we did.

Kate was a good sidekick in Buenos Aires. Originally from the U.S., she spoke Spanish and could roughly translate menus and order for me in a city where English was not widely spoken. At Oui Oui, this wasn't necessary. English was quite common, a brunch *lingua franca*. The four women sitting next to us, in fact, were expat Californians living in Buenos Aires and they discussed celebrity gossip and their busy lives. We bundled ourselves a little better as we sat, watching as people waiting for a seat inside were slowly admitted – parties of three, four, even five people. Most spoke Spanish to each other, indicating they were likely *porteños*, as Buenos Aires locals are known. All restaurant meals are slow in Buenos Aires, so these folks were enduring an extra-long wait, and they became the backdrop to our meal. I had discovered in the week previous that service everywhere in Argentina was slow, and waiters never gave any indication that you needed to move along and vacate your seat, not even offering to bring the bill when you say something definitive like 'I'm done.' At a café or a bar, I started asking for the cheque at the same time I ordered my last drink so that it would come when I was nearly finished. It's a place where leisure is allowed to unfold at, well, a leisurely pace. When experiences are globalized and the same everywhere, the subtle articulation of local culture and behaviours are interesting to watch for, as they indicate there's a strong will and instance upon keeping these particular customs alive.

As it turned out, regardless of Argentina's rich culture and history, the small Oui Oui menu contained items typical of brunch anywhere, with a few local twists: *Croque Madame et Croque Monsieur, bagel con salmon y Philadelphia, pate oui con pan, huevos completos*, and *café Americano* and *mate cocido*. A smaller menu was written out on a narrow chalkboard that hung on one of the plane trees:

PATE

HUMUS

PALTA

QUESOS

PAPAS

SALMON

VINO

CERVEZA

CAMPARI

B MARY

Our server, a young woman dressed as bohemian as any Berlin or New York brunch-slinger, came in and out of the restaurant on occasion, disappearing for five or ten minutes at a time. It was unclear if she was assigned to only the patio or to the interior tables as well. I asked Kate what was vegetarian and ordered a little sandwich on a baguette. Being away from home is one of the acceptable times for day drinking, like being on the beach or during the holidays, when the usual guilt and rules don't apply, so I ordered wine. 'Do you want small or big?' our server asked, and knowing how long this meal would take, I chose big. Big turned out to be a half-litre poured into a teapot-like ceramic decanter that may actually have been a teapot.

There was nothing unpleasant about any of this. The food was good, the day buzz from the wine was all a person could want on an overcast afternoon, and Kate and I had a good long conversation about our backgrounds, careers and the intersection of our lives back in Canada. It was all the things people who enjoy brunch say they get out of brunch. And with much of Buenos Aires shut down on a sleepy Sunday, I didn't feel like I was missing anything except more geography. A good city walk weaves in and out of places of commerce and public-private spaces, so when most of those places are closed it is considerably less exciting and my usual anxiousness to see more was not as acute.

And yet as good and relatively quick as our brunch was – in part because we sat on the slightly too-cold patio rather than waiting in the non-line line – it gave us a front-row view of the quiet suffering the other brunchers were going through. We saw them look up with desperate anticipation each time the hostess came out, cast her gaze left and right with what seemed like a dramatic pause designed to heighten tension and called out a name. The winners didn't show too much excitement when called – that would indicate the line was an issue – and the losers slowly turned their heads back to each other, shifted their weight, leaned up against one of the plane trees or absently kicked a piece of Buenos Aires' notoriously deteriorating sidewalks. As quiet as Sunday is in this city, forced loitering for half an afternoon is still a waste of time. Meanwhile, outside of Palermo Soho, unfashionable but still quite lovely cafés prepared breakfasts and lunches, perhaps not advertised on cute chalkboard menus, that were served by middle-aged waiters in suit and tie rather than hip young servers, and to people who didn't wait in line and were in and out as quickly as Buenos Aires society permits. These cafés, plentiful in many districts of the city, are the equivalent of the hotel brunch, traditional places to eat that work and have a lot of style, but aren't of the moment, and certainly aren't written up in the *Wallpaper* guide. Fashion has moved on from this decidedly Evita style.

That one can find so much of both that old school (or 'old world') style that remains present in Buenos Aires, and the new fashionableness that places like Oui Oui represent, was remarkable in light of what the country had been through in recent decades. Though the Argentine economy is recovering slowly, those crumbling sidewalks underneath the people waiting for a table shouldn't be overlooked. As grand as large parts of Buenos Aires are, and it is an immense city of around 11 million people, there's a feeling of faded glory there, and moving through the city is to walk among the beautiful decay of a once-powerful economy that had produced a robust middle class and attendant culture, but was now holding on to the tropes of a lifestyle as best it could. This isn't meant to overly simplify a complex city and economy; it's a place that has vast working-class neighbourhoods and a brand-new port district, Puerto Madero, that has undergone a massive regeneration like similar areas in Hamburg or London have, complete with designs by superstar architects, including a bridge by Santiago Calatrava and the Philippe Starck–designed Faena Hotel that was created in a turn-of-the-last-century industrial building. It's a jet-set and super-yacht kind of place, but only a short walk from a vast *villa miseria* – a shanty town like the more well-known *favelas* in Brazil that translates to 'miserable city' – next to the main railway station. So there are extremes here too, but it's those expansive middle-class neighbourhoods I found unexpectedly interesting.

Buenos Aires has neighbourhood after neighbourhood of smart apartment buildings that seem at once Parisian and Upper

East Side Manhattan, as well as homes in lower-rise areas that range from small villas (and some big ones too) to what are essentially row houses, the equivalent of a New York brownstone. It was at a casual barbecue at a modest villa owned by the parent of one of the artists participating in the symposium that I learned property was an investment that had stayed solid throughout the crisis, a pillar of middle-class sensibility that remained, as did this household's memory of an older Argentina, represented by the portrait of Evita that hung in an upstairs hallway. Throughout these neighbourhoods people dressed smartly, and there were many more scarves tied in elaborate knots around necks in the chilly fall weather. Middle-class people like their elaborately tied scarves. Dog walkers were plentiful and would tie up their brood of well-coifed canines outside a building while they went up to collect another (Buenos Aires has the most poodles I've yet encountered, more so than even Paris). Café patios were plentiful, as were the bookstores. In fact, this was the most bookish city I've been to, with many traditional stores found on retail streets and book-selling kiosks that set up in the middle of boulevards and at open-air markets selling not pulp but literature and non-fiction. Certainly signs of a strong intellectual culture, but they may also be unintentional if lovely vestiges of an economy that was slow to adopt broadband technologies that, in other places, have put physical bookstores out of business.

Most of all, there was an enjoyment of life in Buenos Aires that seemed oblivious, or perhaps more rightly defiant, in the face of those crumbling sidewalks. I'm not generally an enthusiastic restaurant-goer — if there's an antonym to the dreadful word *foodie*, I am it — but even I enjoyed going out to dinners in this food-happy culture, with multiple courses and the cheapest bottles of great wine around (a roughly glass-to-bottle equivalent between North America and Argentina prices). Though it's a meat-centric cowboy nation, even a vegetarian like myself can get along just fine on their massive ensaladas that came with a meal's worth of vegetables and more, though I was sometimes questioned if I'd have enough to eat. It's a culture that knows how to enjoy itself publicly, and one that places such a high value on this lifestyle, it's clearly a glass-floor item, something that can't and won't be given up, even if it's at odds with the state of the economy. And, as Kate and I discovered, the typical urban North American–style brunch, with all of its time-wasting and self-flagellating aspects, has taken root here too, within this larger culture of middle-class enjoyment, right down to the last detail.

Reflecting on it later, I was reminded of my graduate work studying liberation theology as a transnational social movement, a theory and practice that began in Latin America in the poorest parts of Catholic parishes. Adherents to liberation theology took to heart biblical notions of helping the poor and were using the Church itself as a means of empowering – liberating – the impoverished. That is, until the movement's popular spread was stamped out in the 1980s due to its often overtly Marxist tendencies, something the current Pope, Francis, saw during his time as a local priest in Argentina (he is now seemingly making amends for his lack of action during that era). Despite the crackdown, some of the movement's flames did manage to keep burning, one of them being the North American sanctuary movement that was taking in Central American refugees who were fleeing regimes supported by the U.S. government. Churches in the United States and Canada provided sanctuary for people who were unofficially recognized as refugees, putting those providing the sanctuary in legal harm as they were harbouring illegal aliens. I looked at how people in those North American churches, not all of them Catholic, found common cause with those in Latin America, seeing themselves as part of the same liberation theology movement, though their backgrounds and geographic locations were different. In connecting the North American sanctuary movement with liberation theology, I investigated a school of sociology that explained how social movements spread transnationally, between groups of people and individuals who had little direct contact with one another, yet who rallied around the same causes. These connections were often fostered by the same trade winds created by globalization, linking people around common ideals and struggles, even when their bonds were loose. Despite the geography and different circumstances, people in North America saw themselves as part of the same movement as those trying to change living conditions in small Brazilian villages or Argentinean slums.

Bear in mind I was researching and writing in the late 1990s, when the Internet did exist but well before it reached the incredible, unrelenting level of global connectedness it has since achieved, and writing about events that largely played out in the 1980s, when the web was still Al Gore's dream. That I was consuming a Buenos Aires brunch in a country that was one of the epicentres of liberation theology was purely coincidental, but it did hasten the connection for me. If the near-identical customs of brunch could spread to Argentina, there's little to stop a sense of class identity and consciousness from forming between brunchers here and elsewhere, just as liberation theology and its sense of mission did two or three decades ago, when we relied on limited analog forms of communication. The brunching class is global, more than a century after this troublesome meal was first imagined as an escape from the rigours of formal class traditions, and just as this food trend travelled far, so could collaborative connections between these creative middle-class people along the same networks.

What Is Brunch Anyway?

In 1895, the English writer Guy Beringer published an essay titled 'Brunch: A Plea' in a now-obscure periodical called *Hunter's Weekly*. Nearly a hundred and twenty years later, the vision for a new meal that he proposed is as real now as a traditional Sunday roast was in his time. Little can be gleaned about Beringer himself – all searches for further information circle back only to this essay. In a 1998 *New York Times* article, 'At Brunch, the More Bizarre the Better,' author William Grimes attributed the invention of brunch to Beringer and quoted a few passages from the original essay: 'Brunch is cheerful, sociable and inciting. It is talk-compelling. It puts you in a good temper, makes you satisfied with yourself and your fellow beings, it sweeps away the worries and cobwebs of the week.'

Just like we do today, Beringer saw the link between brunch and the hangover, writing that having the first meal later in the day on Sunday would make life easier on 'Saturday-night carousers.' Beringer differentiated brunch from those English roasts, calling the latter 'a post church ordeal of heavy meats and savory pies' while brunch, served around noon, would instead begin with tea or coffee, marmalade and other breakfast fixtures, before moving on to heavier fare. 'More than a century later, Beringer's template for brunch remains as valid as the day it was created, perhaps because, in drafting his culinary declaration of independence, he was not overly specific about what dishes should be served,' wrote Grimes. 'He demanded "everything good, plenty of it, variety and selection." In a postscript, he suggested that beer and whisky could be served instead of coffee and tea, laying down a precedent for the mimosa, the Bloody Mary and the screwdriver.' Satisfaction, a little gluttony and a buzz – the familiar components of most brunches served today.

For someone so prescient, even visionary, Beringer is a surprisingly obscure figure. Farha Ternikar hasn't been able to find out any more about him. Ternikar's a professor at Le Moyne College in Syracuse, New York, and author of the recent *Brunch: A History*. Even a call to the British Library didn't help: 'They have a copy of that *Hunter's Weekly*,' she tells me, 'but they won't let anyone touch it because it's so rare.' Ternikar's had more luck with brunch research closer to home. 'American historians and academics often cite New York, Chicago and New Orleans as the first big brunch cities in the United States,' she says. 'New York City because there's anecdotal evidence of Emily Post brunching at Delmonico's in the 1920s. New Orleans had a very early brunch culture, where it was almost like a second breakfast. And there's evidence that in the jazz era Chicago had early brunches as well.' By the 1950s, she says, Americans began to have brunches at home and then, by the 1970s and 1980s, with the rise of conspicuous consumption, brunch began to appear at popular hotels, diners and franchise restaurants. 'We get these real brunch scenes,' she says, 'specifically in large urban centres like Toronto, London, New York and Chicago. And, of course, Portland as well.' (*Portlandia*, Fred Armisen and Carrie Brownstein's affectionate sketch comedy send-up of the Oregon city's strenuously twee, often self-enamoured culture, dedicated the season finale of its second season to a satire of Portland's absurd brunch milieu.)

Ternikar didn't initially set out to write a book about brunch. Her initial interest, developed during a sabbatical two years ago, was in how food and identity intersect, especially with regards to immigrant populations, as food is a gateway to multiculturalism, though limited as it is. Indeed, in a city like Toronto that publicly and officially prides itself on its multiculturalism, that multiculturalism often manifests itself only in the city's dizzyingly eclectic culinary landscape. For many 'white' North Americans, so-called ethnic cuisine can provide a safe, pseudo-relationship through which one can experience 'exotic' cultures without any meaningful, deep interaction with those cultures. How many times have we seen politicians, looking for instant connections to a particular ethnic community, use that community's restaurants or cultural events as a convenient backdrop? (The cheeky name of the Toronto-based web magazine *Ethnic Aisle*, which wittily explores ethnicity and race throughout the city and country, alludes to a related ghettoization in grocery stores.)

Ternikar grew up in Tampa, Florida, a mid-sized city a little bigger than Windsor, though lacking its industrial base. When she left for graduate school in Chicago, which had and continues to have an extensive brunch scene, she noticed the same difference I did between brunch back home and brunch in her new city. In Tampa and Windsor, brunch was held in hotels and banquet halls, both of which maintained a faded, old-school glamour, big rooms that conjured up images of Friars Club roasts and boozy Dean Martin types. They connoted *fancy*. Meanwhile, in Chicago and Toronto, new and trendy brunch spots were decorated in ways that suggested the exact opposite: industrial brick walls, mismatched furniture and what seemed like a conscious rejection of standardization and mass production. The quirky and unique were prized, even if those quirks could be found, as I've discovered, in similar restaurants around the world.

There was also a strange desire to be in environments that seemed older and alluded to a working-class life, sans the smell of sweat – turn-of-the-century factories with that exposed brick and reclaimed wood tables, augmented perhaps with an industrial implement or two hung on a wall. In Windsor (and, I imagine, in Tampa), when an occasion rolled around that was special enough to celebrate with brunch, you wanted to celebrate in style, in an atmosphere a bit more luxurious than what you were used to. You didn't want to spend your off-hours in a place that resembled, no matter how fancifully, the factory or warehouse you slaved in during the day.

'In smaller and working-class cities, people still go to brunch at the nicest place they can afford, whether it's the Sheraton or IHOP,' Ternikar says. 'In bigger urban centres, brunch is a way to seem distinct or cool or hip.' For some people, Ternikar points out, where they eat signals who they are or who they want to be, and that status and distinction is linked to that which is difficult to access. So brunches with ninety-minute waits or where you have to get reservations in advance offer us more status. It's simple economics: scarcity makes something more valuable. The places that are easier to access, like breakfast at McDonald's or brunch at the Hilton or golf clubs that are designed for efficiency, comfort and effortlessness have little status. At Chicago's Alinea, a favourite example of Ternikar's and a restaurant named the best in the

United States by *Gourmet* in 2006, you have to make reservations six weeks ahead.

Restaurant owners, like nightclub owners and H&M, know the value of exclusivity and scarcity. Just as your taste in clothes, music and hobbies shapes your identity, so too can your affection (or distaste) for particular kinds of brunch – where you eat and what you eat while you're there – signal what kind of person you are. Status – our sense of being cool, fitting in and feeling content, all of which contribute to our identity – is connected to the things we consume because they are often our most visible and conspicuous personal choices.

Beloved, once-working-class urban areas like Toronto's Kensington Market, New York's Lower East Side and Williamsburg, or London's Hackney have been transformed into places that maintain the general aesthetic of their working-class roots but perform a much more complicated role in the lifestyle of middle-class people. There's a reason so many brunch places have such a distinctly rough-edged aesthetic: plain wooden chairs, worn wood reclaimed from barns, the substantial bill for the experience tucked into an old mason jar: they are all artifacts of the real. They lend an experience that's highly performative, artificial and under a utilitarian sheen of authenticity. They say, *This is a real experience, connected and rooted, not concocted*. Physicality is important; it provides connections to people who did things and to actual objects that age and alter. It's a strange kind of ju-jitsu – a rejection of the trappings of middle-class life in favour of a more expensive and cleaner simulation of working-class life.

Thorstein Veblen goes into detail about the desirability of a hand-wrought spoon, just as serviceable as one made by the machines of his day, but the effort put into it makes the spoon beautiful and 'some one-hundred times more valuable' than a more common spoon. 'The case of the spoon is typical,' he writes. 'The superior gratification derived from the use and contemplation of costly and supposed beautiful products is, commonly, in great measure a gratification of our sense of costliness masquerading under the name of beauty. Our higher appreciation of the superior article is an appreciation of its superior honorific character.'

Marks of honorific costliness can mean beauty, even if an aesthetic analysis suggests they aren't beautiful, and possibly are ugly, just as time wasted at brunch can be viewed as time well-spent. Patchwork Gucci sweaters from the 1980s, the kind Bill Cosby had a penchant for, and other contemporary couture items routinely found on racks at high-end boutiques and department stores that have no relation to the purchasers' personal style, but are consumed because they are authentically expensive, are part of a tautology that drives people to buy things they don't look good in, and waste time they don't have.

Thinking about the industrial brunch aesthetic, keeping in mind the vague and broad definition of what the middle class is, it's as if the rougher working-class markers are being appropriated as a kind of shared identity because the working class is, historically, so rooted to place, physical products and manual labour, all quite *real* things. The working class also has an identity with an immediate sense of solidarity with other working-class people, so this aesthetic suggests being part of something bigger. The creative class does so much work that is ephemeral, on computers and via email, in surroundings that don't seem like work at all and spread across so many industries, there is no common, easily recognizable *look* to the work. An open laptop may come close, but is that work or is that Facebook time? The incredible veneration of older working-class trappings suggests in the absence of a consciousness of its own, this class has appropriated another's, though the salt of the earth does not actually get on one's shoes.

Another demonstrative thrust of Veblen's theory with regards to brunch is the conspicuous consumption of goods, a leisure-class requirement. Veblen immediately points to a dietary connection, where status is 'best seen in the use of intoxicating beverages and narcotics,' he writes. 'If these articles of consumption are costly, they are felt to be noble and honorific.' A mark of honour today is the risky thrill of badass bacon.

'Brunch is a reason for bad behaviour,' Ternikar tells me. 'If you look at the history of brunch, it was the one time no one will judge you if you order an alcoholic beverage before noon and it's the time no one will judge if you want to have bacon and cake at eleven o'clock with your favourite cocktail.' Behaviours that are considered vice, for Veblen, are marks of superior status and 'become virtues and command the deference of the community,' a kind of physical endurance like sport, but where you get less healthy instead of fitter, though your esteem among others rises. Think of a socially acceptable and more couth version of John Belushi's Bluto from the film *Animal House*. 'Drunkenness and other pathological consequences of the free use of stimulants therefore tend in their turn to become honorific, as being a mark, at the second remove, of the superior status of those who are able to afford the indulgence,' writes Veblen. 'Infirmities induced by over indulgence are among some peoples freely recognised as manly attributes. It has even happened that the name for certain diseased conditions of the body arising from such an origin has passed into every speech as a synonym for "noble" or "gentle,"' Veblen isn't specific about which disease, but this notion is reminiscent of how gout was considered the 'the disease of kings and the king of diseases,' and a sign of living the good life. T-shirts announcing one's cholesterol count might sell well outside the hottest brunch spots.

Food has become a conspicuously rebellious act. We've seen a rise of extreme eating that is closely associated with brunch in the form of obsessively meaty charcuterie restaurants, restaurants that flout safety regulations by serving raw pork and, of course, all of that bacon. Bacon is a celebrated, almost cigarette-like food that is sexy and deadly but now part of the ritual intake of grease on a Sunday morning to ease a hangover, just like having smoke and a coffee once were. The unhealthiness of the food is a value-added factor in the experience, another bit of real. The unhealthier the food, the greater the opportunity to boast of said activity on social media. When the cracks in the glass bottom of class sensibility are out of view, do we need to manufacture risk to have a foil to play against?

Or course, playful risk like this comes in working-class forms too – a Toronto greasy-spoon dive called Dangerous Dan's serves a burger called 'the Big Kevorkian,' named after the assisted-suicide crusader – but there's something more forthright about other kinds of bad-for-you food rituals. Dangerous is, well, dangerous: the risks are clear and aren't cloaked in 'authentic' or 'artisanal' euphemisms. And certainly at those Windsor banquet halls and hotels there was a tray of bacon, but it was just bacon, a basic foodstuff rather than a food fetish with an edge and cult following. If someone ate too much of it, they certainly didn't talk about it and there was a safety catch of shame to prevent people from piling it up too high.

Just like having a broad international palate today, where there's pride in one's knowledge and enjoyment of ethnic restaurants that has come to be a surrogate for multiculturalism itself, food is a recreation of the risk that other, working classes face every day. Food is a versatile cultural signifier that can show how badass a person is or how accepting and progressive he is, without having to be particularly badass (or deeply tolerant, in the case of eating multiculturally) in reality. Since the typical urbane bruncher does not work in a profession that is particularly dangerous, like mining or underwater welding (though some people in those vocations likely enjoy a brunch now and then too), and lead urban domestic lives in relatively genteel surroundings, this fetishization of the less healthy aspect of the brunch menu has much in common with extreme sports and ultimate adventures where people opt to inject some managed risk into middle-class stability and safety, while those in working and poorer classes would happily manage more risk out of their lives. Just look at the professions of the people who pay tens of thousands of dollars to climb, and sometimes die on, Mount Everest each year.

Brunch has become an identity its participants embody the way clothes, music choices, hobbies or work can inform self-identity. People often list the enjoyment of brunch in Twitter profiles and on dating web sites as a marker of what kind of person they are; if two people both brunch, they must certainly be compatible (at least they'll be able to talk about the food, and maybe take some pictures). *Brunch* is a code word for a lifestyle where a very specific kind of widely shared leisure is celebrated and sought after, a sensibility summed up in one, easy-to-say, happy-sounding word.

Ivor Tossell, a Toronto friend, wrote a column for the *Globe and Mail* in 2012 called 'Have your cake, but don't tweet it, too,' telling his readers, 'It is time that we had a talk about taking photos of our food.' Ivor goes on to poke a bit of fun at all the Instagramming and tweeting of food pictures, where otherwise smart and socially aware folks might take a picture of a crumbly piece of cake in the bottom of a box and send it out to their equally smart and socially aware followers. His was a fairly kind and benign criticism of the trend, but he received a massive amount of pushback in the comments section and on Twitter itself. People don't like being told that what they're doing is somehow related to class. 'Food isn't just sustenance; it's edible status,' writes Ivor. 'Photographing food is, in the most literal sense, conspicuous consumption. "Look at this nice-looking thing!" says the food photographer. "Someone has put a lot of effort into making it look just so. Guess what I'm going to do with it now?"' As Ivor points out, food is inherently mundane and prosaic, the basic fuel of life, but one that is about much more than just giving us the energy to get through another day. Photographing it, talking endlessly about it and celebrating it are much more about being associated with what's around the food than the food itself, and people don't want to hear that, so Ivor got an earful. Though nobody wants to hear they're performing a socially constructed class ritual, snapping photos connects people who have the loosest ties between each other; it's a way of identifying with each other, even if not intentionally.

Farha Ternikar explains that from a sociological perspective, all notions of authenticity are a social construction, and that what is authentic to some is not authentic to others, so, like class itself, the rules and parameters are subjective for each of us. One person's exotic is another's local. 'There are those who always want to have the most exotic brunch, and who decides what's the most exotic are the people who have the most cultural capital – the tastemakers,' she says. 'You see this in New York all the time with the fashion cycles of food. Who decided that doughnuts are cool again?' She points out how six years ago people were spending ten dollars on artisan cupcakes but now they're lined up for the cronuts in Manhattan, and though there isn't much difference in reality between a cronut in New York or a doughnut in a Tim Hortons or other chain coffee shop, one has, for a limited time, tremendous cultural value and the other does not. Fashion tastes keep things in vogue only briefly, so there is a need to rush out and get it before it's done – a built-in scarcity. Then it's on to the next, newer thing, and the cycle continues.

Veblen saw this too, that the highest value was placed on the desire of the moment. 'The prevailing fashion is felt to be beautiful,' he writes. Explaining further, Veblen says the value of something is due partly to the relief of its being different from what went before it. Humans are creatures of perpetual motion, and though conservatism can be a strong current in a macro sense, we often desire change at a micro level to keep life interesting. Change can come in the form of new pants or maybe a different way of making a grilled cheese sandwich. The new thing that is in fashion assumes an inherent reputability, and though unearned, the ever-changing canon of what's reputable shapes our tastes. 'Under its guidance anything will be accepted as becoming until its novelty wears off, or until the warrant of reputability is transferred to a new and novel structure serving the same general purpose,' writes Veblen. 'That the alleged beauty, or "loveliness," of the styles in vogue at any given time is transient and spurious only is attested by the fact that none of the many shifting fashions will bear the test of time. When seen in the perspective of half-a-dozen years or more, the best of our fashions strike us as grotesque, if not unsightly.' Veblen's late-Victorian-era fashion trends behaved the same way trends do today, where we get a kick out of the clothes we wore and the haircut we sported a decade earlier. Veblen calls this 'aesthetic nausea,' and in the case I'm about to describe, a food item went quickly out of fashion with some physical nausea too.

The cronut burger landed in Toronto during the summer of 2013 at the Canadian National Exhibition, a fair that takes place the last two weeks of August each summer. Whereas the CNE was once a place where new technologies like the television and the electric railway were introduced to the general public, now the big media story each year is the stunt food introduced in the food pavilion. Presumably mad chefs working in undisclosed kitchens came up with previous food fantasies like the Krispy Kreme burger, bacon and Nutella cones, deep-fried butter and even a bacon-wrapped, deep-fried Mars bar. In the run-up to the 2013 exhibition, every media outlet in the city, and some national ones, had stories about the cronut burger, a deep-fried half-dough-nut, half-croissant bun stuffed with meat and cheese and topped with maple bacon jam. Once the CNE gates opened, a steady stream of cronut tweets flowed, followed by more news stories – until somebody got sick eating a cronut. In a stunt gone terribly wrong, the cronut was giving people food poisoning, as the maple butter jam was contaminated with staphylococcus aureus, a toxin derived from humans via skin, infected cuts, pimples, nasal passages and the throat. The story could not have a more descrip-tive villain. As people got sick, there was both a sense of *schaden-freude* that they got what they deserved, but also an unsurprised sense of knowing this is how it was always supposed to end, much like when Joan Didion saw Los Angeles on fire from the Harbor Freeway. Extreme food will, inevitably, end with one kneel-ing over a toilet.

Though the hype around the annual CNE stunt food has an air of fun about it, media plays a big role in constructing the artifice around brunch too. When I ask her how race, gender and sexuality intersect with brunch, Farha Ternikar says she doesn't think race plays a big role in brunch scenes (though it's easily mocked as a 'Stuff White People Like' pastime), saying it's much more about class. Pointing out that there's no hard research on gender and sexuality among those who brunch, she's noticed anecdotally and through media representations that it is portrayed as a hetero-gendered event, where the 'ladies who lunch' in the 1960s became the 'ladies who brunch' by the 1980s and later were depicted in television shows like *Sex and the City*. During the pros-perous post-war era, she traces post-war brunch trajectory-fuelled conspicuous consumption that moved from the home in the 1950s out into public, as hotels, diners and other restaurants began to serve brunch, probably not unlike the ones I grew up with in Windsor, though in large urban centres like Toronto, London,

New York and Chicago, brunch scenes had developed by the time Carrie Bradshaw and her Manolo Blahniks walked in to meet her pals at the latest midday Manhattan hot spot.

'The way the American media represents brunch, which I'm not sure is accurate, is that brunch is something that is still gendered and classed,' says Ternikar. 'In the show *How I Met Your Mother*, there's a whole episode where one of the characters is single and wanted to go to brunch and his friends said to him, "Dudes don't brunch," so there's a gendered stereotype, and I'm not sure it's true because there's been no sociological study actually looking at men vs. women brunching.' Indeed, based on my own anecdotal line-watching and Twitter and Instagram following in Toronto and beyond, brunch doesn't seem to have firm limitations and is as gay as it is straight, attended by middle-class men and women of all persuasion.

Thus Ternikar outlines that brunch is just another mode of consumption for the middle class, and since consumption of fashionable items is linked so closely to identity, food has become another way to consume what we think is authentic. 'In the 1980s,' says Ternikar, 'people wanted to have designer clothes, but by the 1990s if you were really in the know you bought artisanal clothes from independent artists, and now food follows these fashion trends, so when we think about authenticity and identity and brunch, for some people where they eat signals who they are or who they want to be.' She says the so-called foodies often only want to eat food they think is authentic. Sometimes this means finding an authentic brunch that is local or organic or artisan, where the pedigree of the chicken is known (another aspect of brunch that *Portlandia* skewered).

These are powerful trends generating an enormous amount of media that disseminates what's in fashion and where the hottest brunch is, an ever-changing Top 5 list, a process that is self-immolating because once it is too popular it will likely fall off the list. Finding out where the hip brunch places are, and appreciating expensive farmers' markets, the right neighbourhoods and all the other attendant lifestyle tropes of the modern leisure class that go along with this pursuit of fashion, is a particular kind of aspirational cultural capital, different from what the very rich or traditional middle class has developed, explains Ternikar. The creative class has eschewed the old expressions of affluence, the mansions and expensive cars, for lifestyle experiences like food, investing in finding artisanal, organic or local food to create and strengthen their identity. Along the way they are amassing social and cultural capital by listening to the coolest music, having the best brunches and other similar endeavours that are analogous to Veblen's notion of conspicuous consumption, which also requires investing in connoisseurship. Identity creation takes considerable effort.

'The quasi-peaceable gentleman of leisure, then, not only consumes of the staff of life beyond the minimum required for subsistence and physical efficiency, but his consumption also undergoes a specialization as regards the quality of the goods consumed,' Veblen writes. 'He consumes free and of the best, in food, drink, narcotics, shelter, services, ornaments, apparel, weapons and accoutrements, amusements, amulets, and idols or divinities.' Members of the creative class have become experts in the minutiae of craft beer, can describe the bouquet of a wine vintage and know the genealogy of rock bands the way an obsessed baseball fan can recite a favourite player's stat history, and one will, when not enjoying leisure, busy themselves in what Veblen calls the 'business of learning' as they cultivate increasingly refined aesthetic faculties at wine tastings and by reading up on the pedigree of heirloom tomatoes. His list of the kinds of knowledge that are valued by the leisure class can be easily mapped to present-day equivalents. 'So, for instance,' Veblen writes, 'in our time there is the knowledge of the dead languages and the occult sciences; of correct spelling; of syntax and prosody; of the various forms of domestic music and other household art; of the latest proprieties of dress, furniture, and equipage; of games, sports, and fancy-bred animals, such as dogs and race-horses.'

The connoisseur strives for what's new and unique, while a more traditional kind of conspicuous consumption goes for an unchanging style. 'There are two kinds of trends, the super hipster brunch where you want to go to the place that has the smallest number of tables and everything is artisan and local and perhaps vegan, but there is still an attraction for some people, with maybe new money, to go to the big extravagant hotel brunch or even the historical brunch places,' says Terniker. 'For example, brunch in London at the Wolseley is considered an institution, but tourists and celebrities go there. Same thing in N.Y. and Chicago – people still brunch at the Waldorf Hotel in New York or the Drake Hotel in Chicago, but if you're really cool you find the next on-trend brunch place in Brooklyn, because all the cool people brunch in Brooklyn, not in Manhattan.' Terniker also points out how quickly brunch trends can travel to and from places as disparate as Chicago, Dubai and Mumbai, with cronuts and culturally hybrid foods criss-crossing the ocean like jet-set notions gobbled up by customers who are fiercely independent and non-conformist, but who are doing the same thing people are doing elsewhere. All those people shuffling their feet in line at Oui Oui in Buenos Aires could find a home in which to shuffle in cities around the world. Time is wasting everywhere.

Places like the Waldorf or Drake, even though they're desired by wealthier people, tend never to appear on the Top 10 lists, while the creative class, many of whom make much less money and have precarious employment, enjoy, at least, the spoils of social capital that come with being tastemakers, and attend the restaurants that do get the attention. Too bad social capital can't be transferred into a pension or property.

The members of the middle class who seek out brunch experiences like this are members of the modern-day version of Veblen's leisure class. While the very affluent may choose the fancier hotels as they cannot be bothered with the wait and the mercurial service, they operate in a different sphere of social markers and don't need to be seen at the hottest spots in order to confirm their identity and status. The brunching class has instead dropped a desire for the pomp and circumstance of the fancy brunch for one that references an industrial working life, without the work itself, yet the actual work that goes into making brunches happen is conspicuously left out of the celebrated brunch narrative, even though it's often happening in plain view.

Inside
the Brunch Machine

As seemingly removed as it is from work and worry, like many leisure pursuits, brunch doesn't just happen on its own; there is an elemental physical labour necessary to make it happen. Behind the swinging kitchen doors, or in restaurants with open kitchens, right before your very eyes, there is grease, sweat, noise, heat and something called the dish pit. 'The dish pit is the backbone of brunch, as far as I'm concerned,' Rachael Popowich tells me. She's a cook at Aunties & Uncles, a Toronto brunch spot where she started as a dishwasher. 'It's absolutely unrelenting, a different kind of job than any other, because all you're doing is bringing the situation back to neutral. And you do that over and over again. At least when you're in the kitchen and you're cooking, you put something up on the pass [the counter between the kitchen and dining room], there's the satisfaction of thinking, "I made that. Someone is going to eat and enjoy that." Working in the dish pit's more thankless.'

Aunties & Uncles is a quintessential Toronto brunch spot that has perennially been on best-brunch lists since it opened in 1998, a remarkable lifespan for any restaurant (especially one that doesn't serve alcohol). Small and bohemian, with an open kitchen, Aunties & Uncles has a lineup every weekend and was one of the first brunch places I was invited to in Toronto. Popowich has a BA in English and, while looking for a job in a creative field, started in the dish pit a year ago. Her uncle owns the place and she's long had a close-up view of life and work there.

I've never worked in any kind of food service and can never figure out how that particular machine works, or how the chaos is kept at bay. There are so many variables: the constant juggling of individual diners' needs and desires, the rapid pace of the kitchen, the delicate chemistry of the cooking itself. Even keeping a factory-floor production line moving didn't produce the same stress. (When that line stopped, somebody else – a mechanic or other skilled tradesperson – would come along and fix it.) As

Popowich describes her experience on the other side of the grill, it sounds like life on a small ship, where everyone works together to keep it moving forward lest it drift into the rocks and sink, but also where the people on the upper decks are blissfully unaware of the effort and stress below decks, even when it's in partial view – nearly as blunt a jump-cut as James Cameron made in *Titanic*, from a Veblen-era leisure crowd to the army below, keeping the coal-fired boilers steaming.

'It's like there's an engine in the basement,' Popowich says. 'That's the prep kitchen. And this is where it can get kind of tense. People have to be more flexible than they would like to be when you're working in a small restaurant … it's about keeping things moving. You're always checking to make sure everything's going in the right direction.' Kitchen staff usually arrive an hour before opening to prepare their 'lines,' or their stations in the kitchen. Popowich is the 'second cook' and makes sweets, pancakes, French toast and grilled sandwiches. Her partner, who she says is 'sort of at the helm of the ship,' does the eggs and meat. Above and below her grill, she keeps her materials – ingredients, condiments, etc. – and constantly monitors their levels. When she's getting low, she'll ask a server to notify the prep kitchen below that she needs more greens or whatever. Focused on customers, however, servers often forget and tensions arise.

It's a small machine, but one with parts that can become quickly irritated. For an average weekend shift, Popowich arrives at 8 a.m. to prep for the nine o'clock opening. On an ideal weekend day, people arrive slowly and begin to fill the restaurant until it's at capacity, staying that way until two or two-thirty, when it finally slows down. She then has a little time to clean up and make staff meals before the restaurant closes at three. Weekdays are less hectic, but on weekends there are no breaks, save for the very few moments when there are no orders up (and if you've ever worked in a unionized environment, you know how sacrosanct breaks are and how transgressive it would be to give them up, but in brunch, and certainly in the patrons' creative-class jobs, break time can evaporate quickly). Then she might have time for a coffee. Staff eat together at the end of the shift, also like the crew on a ship would.

Popowich has done a long and informal sociological study of her brunch patrons. 'There are regulars that are pretty great,' she says, when I ask about her typical customers. 'A lot of University of Toronto students. Moms who've just dropped their kids off at school next door. There are [typical] groupings of customers who come in for brunch too. Two girls who are old friends in the same city, catching up – they're probably going to order one savoury thing and one sweet thing and split it, and drink lots of teas. Groups of guys coming in, hungover, are going to order tons of juices and breakfast pockets and burgers. You can almost see the orders coming in before they come in.'

Echoing what Terniker says about the brunch experience, Popowich thinks the appeal of brunch is customers who want 'a little sizzle with their steak.' That is, an experience. On a weekday, a customer can be in and out of Aunties & Uncles in fifteen minutes; on a weekend they'll have to give up their morning or afternoon for the experience and spend a fair amount of cash on something that's ephemeral. 'It's not a low-class problem, you know?' Popowich says of the sacrifices people make for brunch. The amount of money customers spend on their meals, around twelve or fifteen dollars each, is also about what Popowich makes in an hour. If you've ever worked an hourly job where the pay is relatively low, these kinds of comparisons, of time with an object or commodity, happen all the time. At the record store, making about seven dollars an hour meant it took me two hours to buy a CD that was on sale and three or four hours for something that was regularly priced (iTunes has probably changed the model as the one-dollar increments are harder to *feel*).

It's a depressing way to count the hours, and a way of thinking about money that can limit your brunchlike expenditures. Not just because there isn't that much money to spend on those kinds of activities, but because money and time are related directly to everyday consumer objects and ephemeral experiences. There are dollar signs everywhere. Each CD, even with a modest employee discount, was a precious item, considered for a long time before purchasing. Working in the store, I was fascinated by the casual consumers who would walk in without anything in particular in mind, ask what was good and buy it on the spot. Though I no longer get paid by the hour and I'm comfortable enough to not think as much about the smaller items I might spontaneously buy, I still often shop in the same way, returning to a store to try on clothes or shoes a second or third time, or endlessly reading product reviews online to convince myself something is worth buying. It's a kind of built-in pre-buyer's remorse that sometimes prevents me from falling into fashion traps of buying the shiny thing of the day before thinking about how it fits into my life and style.

At the same time, Popowich says, low income doesn't always prevent brunching, as it's a 'glass bottom' experience that there's always money for. 'A lot of students brunch,' she says. 'A lot of people who don't have a lot of disposable income will choose to use what they do have on brunch, just to feel like, "On my day off, I can dabble in this lifestyle." It's not unlike working-class people spending a lot of money to go to expensive and flashy nightclubs with overpriced drinks and a high cover charge in order to experience a Studio 54–like glamour. It's telling that so many of the dance and house anthems played at these kinds of clubs are all about liberation, forgetting one's troubles and leaving the drudgery behind.

Aesthetically speaking, Aunties & Uncles is closer to a diner, albeit a bohemian version, than a trendy brunch place, so when I ask Popowich to describe what makes a brunch 'brunch' and not breakfast or lunch, her answer is surprising. 'When Aunties & Uncles started, you could order breakfast or you could order lunch,' she says. 'We could give you a burger or a BLT or we could give you bacon and eggs. We didn't do eggs Benedict; we didn't do any of that kind of stuff. But because of the hours of our operation, people called it brunch, and that's what it ended up being. I've gone out to brunch with friends and ordered eggs Benedict and Caesars and had a great time. I almost think that the appeal of going out to do that vs. going to a diner, where one person can order breakfast and one person can order lunch, is that it feels kind of naughty, don't you think? It's like adults getting to be mischievous children. "Ooh, we'll drink at breakfast. Let's be naughty. We're going to spend all this money on eggs and feel fabulous." It's also a bit of conspicuous consumption. People want to go to the popular brunch spot so they can be seen there, because it's also showing people, "I've got money and I've got time.'"

Of Farmers' Markets, Walmart and Condos

'I've got the money and I've got the time' is a prevailing middle-class sensibility, but in an uncritical milieu of consumption, both these notions are at risk. What's more, the same desire for the perfect brunch is connected to other practices that hinge on troublesome class assumptions and feel-good illusions that should be part of any examination of how the middle class live today.

Striving for authenticity extends far beyond the restaurant. For five years, I lived in Cabbagetown, a historic neighbourhood a twenty-minute walk east of downtown Toronto. In the 1960s, the housing stock here – often said to be the largest intact Victorian neighbourhood in North America – went decidedly down-market, in many instances becoming rooming houses with absentee landlords. A decade later, the area was rediscovered by a middle class who bought the homes and transformed the neighbourhood into an exclusive showpiece that you need a six-figure – often seven-figure – mortgage to get into. Cabbagetown remains bookended to the north and south by lower-income neighbourhoods, and the main street that connects all of them, Parliament, is a beguiling blend of the high, the low and the in-between (there are even a few brunch places). On the edge of a river valley, Cabbagetown's Riverdale Park has its own working farm, complete with the standard barnyard stars, and is adjacent to a wonderfully Gothic cemetery, the Toronto Necropolis. In many ways, Cabbagetown is the archetypal neighbourhood, desired by the urban professionals and creative types who reject both the suburbs and contemporary high-rise living. The cows moo into the night, the children play in the wading pool by day, people stroll the calm sidewalks and gawk at the architecture, and bucolic city life carries on, especially during summer.

On Tuesdays, however, cars always surround Riverdale Park, sometimes double-parked, while others crawl along the surrounding narrow residential streets, looking for a spot. There is gridlock. In the park itself, cube vans and small trucks line the edges, some with portable generators buzzing away. These are all signs that the weekly Riverdale Park farmers' market is in full swing, even before the tents and tables are themselves visible. Like a brunch's temporal reach, hogging up time, the farmers' market here has quite a geographic reach.

Not all farmers' markets work the same, and in neighbourhoods with higher densities and more apartment clusters, there may be more people who walk to them – that's presumably the way it's supposed to work. But after a few years of watching the Riverdale Park farmers' market, it didn't seem much different, in practice, from supermarkets that are criticized because people drive to get to them. The difference between the supermarket and this market is that each individual vendor also drives in, whereas supermarkets are stocked through a centralized distribution system in which a few big trucks deliver multiple goods.

On the face of it, farmers' markets are good things. We like food, and we in cities like farmers too, despite the supposed political divide between the urban and the rural (a false, exaggerated divide). There's a long tradition of markets in the city, and many city centres have very famous ones that are as much tourist attractions as they are places where locals shop. Many Canadian small towns started as marketplaces, and more than a few neighbourhoods in cities like Toronto began as market garden locations, where food was grown and sold in the city, a phenomenon that may be slowly returning, albeit in altered form, with the rise of urban farming.

At the weekly Cabbagetown market, as at others like it, the 'farmers' are there too, selling the produce they presumably grew themselves in the nearby hinterland. The experience of meeting the person who grew the food about to be consumed is considered valuable, though it doesn't change the taste or quality of the food. It simply makes people feel good, like they've had an authentic farm-to-fork experience, the agricultural equivalent of exposed brick. One reason people say they like going to their local farmers' market is because they can get to know the person who grows their food. That certainly is a nice sentiment, even if it is girded by nostalgia for a farmer-consumer relationship that rarely existed, if it did at all. Everybody likes new friends, but I wonder if it is simply an urban feel-good thing, a way to convince ourselves that city living is not completely removed from nature and that we're not all cogs in some dystopian technocracy – or so goes the logic that seems to deny the very urbanity of our existence in cities with complex economies. We don't know who designed our computers, who made our clothes or who processes our garbage and sewage. Would our lives be better if we did? Would the products? Likely not. Is the desire for a relationship with our farmers just sentimentality for some old, long-gone and unnecessary way of life? Is the cute farmers' market a desired sensibility that is wholly created for social and cultural reasons, rather than for efficiency and economy?

On the *Freakonomics* blog, James E, McWilliams, a historian at Texas State University and the author of *Just Food: Where Locavores Get It Wrong and How We Can Truly Eat Responsibly*, explored the impulse to strengthen community through farmers' markets. In 2009 he wrote, 'Markets encompass a wide range of experiences. For me, primarily because I don't view the farmers' market as a venue to nurture community bonds, my transactions tend to be as personal or impersonal as if I were shopping at a generic grocery store. Don't get me wrong – I respect my local farmers very much. Still, I approach their stalls not to get to know them, but to buy the excellent food they sell.' He goes on to explain that, historically, local markets were fraught with tension and risk. Everybody knew each other, and they were highly competitive and exclusive.

The exclusive nature of many of the farmers' markets in urban centres is quickly evident when visiting: there are organic dog biscuits that cost $4 each, heirloom tomatoes handled as if they were Fabergé eggs, petite loaves of artisanal bread and tiny jars of homemade jams, chutneys and other prepared foods that have prices not unlike those at boutique foodie emporiums. Sometimes the farmers are new to the game, displaced urbanites who gave up the rat race to become gentleman and gentlewoman farmers, the twenty-first-century version of the baby-boomer back-to-the-landers who made similar migrations in the 1970s. It's a long way from the roadside stand on a country highway, but that's the ideal that many of us have in our minds when we think of these markets. That, outside small rural towns and villages, people still grow things on property that's been in the family for generations, and they make a decent living doing so, and sell some of their produce out front themselves because they love what they do (in that fine country tradition, they often leave a can out by the produce, trusting people to put in their money). The farmers' markets popping up all over urban areas, we're led to believe, are simply an extension of that, a satellite operation straight from the rural mothership. In cities where the bountiful countryside is nearby, this may work just fine, and it certainly does at those large centralized hub markets that see tens of thousands of people on weekend days. But the economics of smaller, quaint farmers' markets are much different, requiring considerable travel, a likely markup of prices and the retail of specialty products arguably more enticing than plain old fruits and vegetables. They are essentially miniature, outdoor versions of Whole Foods. It's boutique produce.

Farmers' markets have become the go-to solution for energizing or re-energizing public spaces and neighbourhoods, and they provide an experience many knowing urbanites will go to great lengths to seek out. These are the urbanites who often profess a strong disdain for run-of-the-mill supermarket chains (and especially Walmart), the kinds of places that a lot of *other* people shop at because they're the only places they can afford or because they simply prefer them. I got an earful of this sentiment when I was on a 2009 panel about food in Toronto. It was held at the Centre for Social Innovation, a co-working space filled with individuals and organizations with social-change mandates, all housed in a converted Victorian warehouse building at the south end of Toronto's main Chinatown. The CSI, as it's known, is the kind of environment now commonly found in cities around the world: an incubator for a host of progressive organizations, techie start-ups and other creative-minded endeavours. The conversation that day ranged from food security to how we get our food on a daily basis. That's where I got into trouble. I started to describe my own experience with farmers' markets and, when I stated that I'd rather shop at No Frills, a discount supermarket two blocks from my house, because it's consistent and not expensive, a woman in the audience shouted, 'How can people eat that – it's not even food!'

There were nods of agreement in the audience, the converted being preached to. 'That makes me feel kind of bad,' I said, 'and angry. I'm pretty sure what I eat is food, and all the other people who I see shopping there must think it's food too.' I said that, just like at farmers' markets, there are often little signs in the produce section at No Frills indicating a foodstuff's provenance – from Ontario in the summer, say, or Mexico in the winter (unless it's grown in a greenhouse, not much grows in Canada in the winter). I also said a lot of the people who shop at the No Frills were from Regent Park, the much less affluent neighbourhood next door. Though I shopped there out of convenience and choice, many people did so because it was the only store they could afford.

Once I had put a human face, or faces, to the behaviour, the woman backed down and even apologized. But her initial outrage was real; the idea that a quotidian discount place, with zero artifice and that is in no way exclusive or aspires to 'authenticity,' could be popular and even beneficial to the local community did not compute. Her confusion is also too common. There's room and need to talk about where our food comes from, how it's produced and who's doing the producing and who's making the money, but over and over, an uncritical, undifferentiated affection for things like farmers' markets blinds us to a true discussion of these issues. It remains unclear why the stalls in the park are superior to the aisles in the store; one is venerated and the other disdained, and there is precious little conversation about what's best for a sustainable food system.

Older neighbourhoods like Cabbagetown have become some of the most cherished neighbourhoods, many with a similar transition story. They are pleasant places to wander; the creative-class gentry gravitate to them as they have an atmosphere Veblen describes as possessing an 'air of leisurely opulence and mastery,' a description that could easily be applied to neighbourhoods with big brunch scenes like the Plateau in Montreal, Williamsburg or

Park Slope in Brooklyn, or half a dozen neighbourhoods in Berlin. A walk through these neighbourhoods, with people sitting in cafés or browsing shops during business hours and in crowded bars until 3 a.m. or later, makes it seem like time is different here, without the usual pressures to get things done. The feeling of mastery comes with the notion that the neighbourhood has evolved to its Platonic ideal and that all is right and good here. But what happens when neighbourhood change continues and rubs against the conservatism that the gentry have also embraced?

In 2013 a Walmart was proposed on the edge of Kensington Market, the most indie and punk rock of all Toronto neighbourhoods, whose narrow streets are occupied by, among other things, an eclectic jumble of greengrocers, army surplus shops, butchers, bars and empanada joints. A slow and steady influx of high-end retailers and restaurants over the last decade have routinely and predictably triggered warnings of gentrification (actual flyers warning of this are slapped on every telephone pole in the neighbourhood when there's a new threat, akin to Cold War air-raid sirens). Kensington Market is exactly the kind of place that mounts campaigns against Walmarts in other cities and towns, analogous to neighbourhoods like Greenwich Village, San Francisco's Mission or Hackney in London: traditionally working-class neighbourhoods that have become playgrounds for the middle class, with just a bare vestige of those working-class roots still visible.

Around the same time the Walmart was proposed, an immense and infamous big-box store called Honest Ed's was quietly put up for sale in a neighbourhood a few blocks north. This retail upheaval inspired a hue and cry from many Torontonians, all of whom lamented its imminent end. To paraphrase another Morrissey song, there was panic on the streets of Kensington. But if someone made a Venn diagram of these two emotional responses, the overlap would have been considerable. The same people who nostalgically mourned Honest Ed's passing were those opposed to Walmart's arrival – one change was a loss for Toronto, the other an attack on it.

Honest Ed's is, and was, a Walmart *avant la lettre*. Founded by a lovable self-made man, Ed Mirvish, sixty-six years ago, the store grew up and out as Toronto did. Eventually festooned with a manic sign a block long with thousands of incandescent bulbs and similarly adorned with quirky, sometimes punning hand-painted signs – 'Honest Ed's is for the Birds … Cheap! Cheap! Cheap!' – it was frequented by generations of working-class and immigrant families. Its quirkiness was beloved, in turn, by hipsters, even if many of them didn't actually shop there. It was a store that became a landmark, a local institution that, though a private enterprise, is treated differently than other businesses because the identity of the surrounding city is so bound to it, like Macy's in New York or Harrods in London. The Mirvish family also helped create and invest in Toronto's big-budget, mainstream theatre scene and have been involved in a number of local philanthropic endeavours, all things that endeared them and their store to the city. Just as food is not always food, a shop is sometimes more than a shop.

Aside from its eccentric design, a garish decorating scheme unchanged since the mid-1970s, there is little difference between Honest Ed's and Walmart. Both sell the same products, many made in foreign sweatshops, and neither have unionized employees. Both also have incredibly big footprints at odds with tightly knit urban areas. These are all criticisms routinely levelled at Walmart. While there's no evidence that the Mirvishes have ever engaged in anti-union activity, and a single store's buying power is, of course, not the same as that of an international chain, the uncritical love Honest Ed's received was curious. The core argument against the Kensington Walmart was that it would destroy the neighbourhood, yet Ed's was of identical scale and function and the surrounding neighbourhood continued to thrive. There is, in fact, an existing Walmart just a few kilometres west of the Market, in a dense, established neighbourhood that has undergone its own modest and largely uncontroversial gentrification. Little outrage greeted that development.

As the debate evolved, here and there a few people warily floated the notion that opposition to the Walmart was classist. They suggested that a lot of people simply prefer to shop at Walmart rather than the jumble of shops and restaurants urbanists cherish and celebrate (and exactly the kind of environment brunch spots find hospitable), because Walmart is cheaper. I say 'warily' because these folks weren't contrarians or Walmart boosters, but they were concerned about how even progressives can overlook the class reasons for the success of Walmart. Walmart has been regularly branded a villain in so many towns and cities across North America that it's almost impossible to imagine good people will ever shop there.

A remarkable thing happened during some of these conversations, something I could not have predicted: when the class issue was brought up, the heads of not a few progressive and lefty folks exploded. It was a conversation-killer, at least in a few of the concentric circles of my Toronto social media world. Some otherwise very nice people became apoplectic when pushed on the class issue, and stormed, as it were, out of the conversation. It just did not make sense to them that working-class people might choose Walmart over Kensington's shops. The one-stop-fits-all of a Walmart has long become the preferred way of shopping for the working and lower-middle classes (and not a few people higher up the rungs). Travelling from small shop to small shop, trying to find bargains that may not be there, takes much more time and effort, and while that might be a kind of ideal for urbanists, it isn't how a lot of people want to spend their time.

Certainly the negative reaction to Walmart is political for many, and justifiably so. In many small towns, Walmart's imperial expansion has decimated traditional downtown shopping areas by offering low prices the independent and smaller retailers can't compete with, and though no fault can be found with people seeking out a cheaper price, the predatory practice has been harmful, creating a monopoly, and it's the reason a Walmart's arrival is something we should be wary of. Walmart's global buying practices are also troublesome, dominating world markets and supply lines and creating industry practices everybody must follow in order to compete, whether it's purchasing sweat-shop products or fighting any attempt at unionization among its own vast workforce.

All of these are legitimate reasons for making a political choice not to shop at Walmart or to actively protest a proposed store, but in larger cities like Toronto there are still ample shopping choices, yet many still opt for the convenience of Walmart. I'm related to some of them, and they aren't monsters. For them, shopping at Walmart, or shopping in general, isn't a political act; in fact, there are no politics to it at all. It's just shopping. Conversely, frequenting local shops and avoiding chains *is* a political choice and, for some, an integral part of their identity (it's easy to conjure the hunting-and-pecking shopper, his or her bike basket well-equipped with canvas bags for his or her native-made and native-grown wares). This is not in any way bad, nor is gently encouraging this kind of indie retail activity in our cities. But the Kensington Walmart response seemed to ignore *who* actually prefers *what* kind of experience, and assumes everybody likes to shop small and has the liberty to make choices based on politics, when small shopping and being choosy is actually a luxury.

Honest Ed's isn't Walmart, it's just one store, but there are enough overlaps in labour, supplier practices and land-use patterns to suggest the free pass Honest Ed's received was related to other sensibilities. Why Walmart is so popular is another worthwhile, but separate, investigation, but I wonder if what I saw was the rough edges of new conceptions of class rubbing up against each other unbeknownst to the participants. Traditional identities or consciousness increasingly don't describe how the real world works in cases like this, as perceptions of who is political and who is not, and who exactly shops where, seem out of alignment with old ideologies. The refusal to even engage in a conversation about this suggests that long-held ideological views of how the world works are extraordinarily difficult to break out of.

If the brunching class came around to seeing their own lifestyle and work life in a more critical way, understanding the nature of their own work, there's potential for better relationships with adjacent, lower classes. A related reshaping of the tectonic plates of class are those knowledge- and creative-class workers who don't identify with the traditional working class, even if their pay and lack of job security is commensurate with older forms of working-class life (Dickens' famous Bob Cratchit, though a working-class icon of the early industrial revolution, was essentially a knowledge worker on a contract job with no security, no benefits and poor pay). Taste and sensibility get in the way of seeing the commonalities among the creative and working classes. Work is work, but even if a creative earns less money than a unionized worker, class becomes a kind of ideology that limits the perception of different kinds of work, failing to allow for cross-class identity, but also limits the conversation around a development like Walmart.

Writing about the Kensington Walmart a few months later in the online magazine *Hazlitt*, another friend, Bert Archer, got to the heart of this fission: 'It's about a pernicious preference for the idea of the working class over the actual members of that class, a refusal to see one's middle-class fetishes as middle-class fetishes.' He goes on, even more emphatically, 'This isn't just a Kensington Market problem: It's a first-world problem. It's our stubborn refusal to look class in the face, to admit that it exists, to realize that only one-third of the Canadian population gets any form of post-secondary education, and that it's the same third whose families earn the most money.' The artifice of class constructions gets in the way of seeing actual class, and produces a myopic kind of class warrior. 'Walmart-hating is easy; class consciousness is not,' Archer concludes.

This is echoed in a July 2013 article, 'Gentrifier? Who, Me? Interrogating the Gentrifier in the Mirror,' in the *International Journal of Urban and Regional Research*. Authors John Joe Schlichtman and Jason Patch examine a tendency in most 'mainstream' *and* 'critical' urbanists to ignore their own role in gentrification and middle-class sensibility. Recounting their own stories of moving into older historic neighbourhoods not unlike Kensington Market, they write, 'There was an *aesthetic* pull of "sentiment and space" to at least some of our neighborhoods: we have no desire to live in the *aesthetic* landscape of uniform subdivisions of postwar aluminum-sided ranches or post-Reagan McMansions nor the class homogeneity that often accompanies them.'

Throughout their article, Schlichtman and Patch aren't arguing that the displacement caused by gentrification isn't a serious urban problem, nor are they condemning the forces that compel middle-class people with what might as well be called a brunching sensibility. Rather, they're simply recognizing how some of these very personal choices might be in conflict with blanket anti-gentrification arguments, and that people should consider how the fruits of gentrification can be reconciled with caring about who gets shut out. I've seen it myself in lefty planner and urbanist friends who get the most upset about affordable housing and hipsters but frequent the new bars and see the bands that inhabit exactly these contested spaces, driving up prices. If experts and the passionate amateurs who are trained to think critically about urbanism can overlook their own complicity in the processes they criticize, then it must be just as easy to obfuscate one's own class sensibility when defending a working-class neighbourhood while rejecting those in it. Somewhere the people get forgotten in the cause, as Bert argues.

The most extreme case of class confusion I've seen in Toronto involves the rapidly gentrifying neighbourhood around Ossington Avenue. Ossington is a dozen or so blocks west of Kensington and, until recently, was a very down-market street comprised of auto-body shops, a detox centre and some sketchy Vietnamese karaoke joints that were the scene of a few violent shootings and kidnappings into the mid-2000s. When I moved to Toronto in 2000, I went to visit a friend from Windsor who lived a half block away from the street. She instructed me to take the streetcar further on and walk up a different route, as Ossington was 'not very nice.' Not dangerous in the *Death Wish* sense – this was still Toronto, after all, an incredibly safe city relative to its size – but it was as rough-and-tumble as downtown Toronto got.

Today, the strip has radically altered, and in the fourteen years I've lived here, Ossington has probably undergone more change, more quickly, than any other neighbourhood I'm aware of here. The detox centre is still there, a battened-down gothic vision housed in a former fire hall, but the karaoke bars are gone, replaced by bars that people line up outside of on weekends and restaurants that are written up (over and over) in the lifestyle magazines and blogs. A condo presentation centre on nearby Queen Street – the temporary building that's created to sell potential residents on the condo that will one day arrive – boldly used the words 'RAW ORGANIC UNSCRIPTED' in its signage, never mind that at least two of those things violate Toronto building codes. Today you can buy $300 jeans on Ossington and, of course, wait in line for brunch on Sundays. The urban fabric along the street is still pleasantly mixed and there remain a few storage depots and garages (as one writer put it a few years ago, Ossington is a place where you can still get a tire fixed).

On the site of one former garage, an eight-storey 'mid-rise' condo building was proposed in 2012. In some Toronto neighbourhoods, this would seem downright stubby, but it was well within the Paris-like height and density ideal that Toronto should be encouraging. On Ossington, however, it would be the tallest building, and, as with many developments in Toronto, there was local opposition. This development, like any in the city, wasn't perfect and needed tweaking so as to better fit into the neighbourhood. But the virulent response to it, on the part of a handful of homeowners, was shockingly intense, attacking not only the proposed condo itself, but the kind of people who might live in it and the few writers who thought the development was a good idea.

The irony was that the us-against-them language used was very David and Goliath, the little guy vs. the developers. The little guys in this case, however, were people who had purchased a formerly working-class home in a formerly modest neighbourhood for hundreds of thousands of dollars because they wanted to live in a neighbourhood that had become hot and trendy. They were the very people complicit in Ossington's transformation, cranking up home prices and changing the nature of retail on the main street. Now they were demanding that the street be frozen in time and that these transformations stop – access to Ossington, they were implicitly saying, should be limited to people like them, with the means to purchase one of the neighbourhood's now-overpriced freehold homes, so the barrier to neighbourhood entry was many hundreds of thousands of dollars rather than a few hundred thousand. Neither are particularly inexpensive, but condos, apart from whatever else they might do, provide somewhat cheaper homes for people a few rungs down the economic ladder. This is not affordable housing by any means, but condos can certainly serve as starter homes for some, places where a single person or couple with good jobs can buy downtown and live, as the opponents of the development do, someplace hip and appealing.

In short, their actions would turn Ossington into an exclusive brunch place that only they knew about and could afford, saying no to what is arguably good change while failing to recognize their own culpability in why people want to move there too. A reset of class identity is needed so we have a more honest appreciation of who we are and how our own behaviours, tastes and desires affect others.

The Portland
Brunch Club

If the brunching class is to recalibrate its notion of class, the easy part is fixing brunch itself. Not going is always an option, but for those who still wish to make an overt statement of leisure and declare a portion of their day work-free, a group of brunchers are taking the mystique, and mistakes, out of brunch and (re)turning it into an enjoyable meal again. It's happening in the unlikeliest of places too – Portland, Oregon, where the *Portlandia* ridiculousness is being avoided for a relaxing kind of brunch everybody expects, but so often doesn't get. The trick, it seems, is rules.

Jen Delos Reyes is a professor of art and social practice at Portland State University. A self-described reformed bruncher, she now makes brunch at home twice a month, for herself, her husband and neighbours. Her admittedly unhealthy menu items could be found in any number of trendy *boîtes*: duck-fat pancakes, collard greens, French toast composed of croissants. Reyes stopped going to brunch largely because she wasn't willing to wait an hour each time she wanted to eat. 'That's one of the reasons I started doing it at home instead,' she says. 'I want to spread out my time in a way that's really relaxing and just shift gears a bit.' Brunch for her is a way to stop working, to really enjoy weekends and engage with other people. There's a no-work rule in effect; phones are kept off and mimosas are served.

Reyes describes the ideal that so many brunch enthusiasts seem to chase, an oasis of relaxation rather than the cesspool of stress it's become. Rachael Popowich, the cook at Aunties & Uncles, speaks similarly, even after outlining the controlled chaos and high stress of her workplace. 'There is a low-pressure element to brunch,' she says. 'My friend Katie works at a law firm and gets very little time off. So when she has a day off, she wants to see her friends, she wants to eat. And there's something about having tentative plans to do brunch that has a relaxing spirit.'

This relaxing spirit is captured by another group of Portlanders who formed what they call the Joy Brunch Club two years ago.

'We meet every Sunday at ten and we try to go to a variety of places that we haven't been before,' says Kate Bingaman-Burt, a graphic-design professor, illustrator and one of the Joy Brunch Club members. 'We don't like to wait in lines, so anyplace that's too popular we don't really like to go to because we think waiting is bullshit. We have this whole system of brunch-club rules that we follow. It gets pretty dorky. We have our own hashtag. It's very fun. It's sometimes the highlight of my week. It's just a really wonderful thing to look forward to.' Bingaman-Burt has been doing a daily drawing since 2006, often featuring brunch items, that is posted on her web site.

The Joy Brunch Club rules mandate that meals begin at 10 a.m. and end no later than eleven-thirty or twelve, sometimes even finishing in an hour, so no sprawling, whole-day-killing brunches. 'One of the things we do at brunch is talk about what we're going to be doing for the rest of the day or what's coming up in our week,' says Bingaman-Burt. 'It's almost a time to process the things that we're looking forward to, the things that we're going to be doing. Sometimes the only time I see that group of friends is on Sundays. I feel like we have a fairly productive brunch club. It doesn't take over the day.'

Each member has veto power over suggested restaurants. The five core members can bring guests with them, but there can't be more than six people at a given meal. This is both to prevent a shared conversation from splintering and to limit the difficulty of finding a restaurant that can accommodate a party of that size. Everyone needs to be consulted on who the guests are, but moms are always welcome. They frown on people from Portland joining as guests, preferring visitors to take the open spot. Whenever somebody is out of town, even if only two are left, the other spots can be filled with guests, and the club has been continuous every Sunday since it began. The hashtag, #joybrunchclub, is a way of letting those who are away share in the experience, albeit with some irony. 'We make fun of it,' Bingaman-Burt says. 'Taking a photo of your food before you eat it is like the new saying grace. We fully realize that it's silly and tongue-in-cheek. But my friend Lisa was in Florida last weekend and tagged a photo of what she was eating. It was kind of like, "We're there with you when you're eating, and you're here with us."' If phones are out too much, however, members are gently chastised.

The Joy Brunch Club began at a Portland establishment called the Nightlight, which Bingaman-Burt describes as a casual place that is a bar by night but by day serves traditional food like eggs, bacon and toast, but, just as importantly, has big circular booths. This was the petit déjeuner of epiphanies: a brunch place at the epicentre of brunch culture that didn't have long lines and offered patrons booths to sit in, bringing this fashion-plagued meal back into diner territory, where functionality trumps the artifice and a good time with friends is the focus. It's still a brunch rather than breakfast or lunch, existing within the Venn diagram of the two meals, but like Aunties & Uncles in Toronto, which didn't set out to become a brunch joint, it's been adopted as one by its patrons.

It's the weekly two-hour ritual that Bingaman-Burt most enjoys, seeing the same people, catching up and simply enjoying a brief respite from work in a life that always feels rushed and busy. 'It's like inhabiting this in-between space that is very deca- dent and luxurious,' says Lisa Ciccarello, another member of the Joy Brunch Club. 'Your level of participation is very low and unhur- ried. I think we've only waited as a group in a long line maybe twice. If we can't get seated within twenty minutes of showing up, we won't go there or we'll leave if it looks like the line is long. For us, there's no mystique about waiting in an hour-long line to eat food. We just really want to eat "almost-breakfast" together every week.'

Like the cliché of good fences making for good neighbours, adherence to the rules keeps brunch close to its ideal state of leisure. 'I don't have any other meal that lasts that long during the week,' says Bingaman-Burt. 'I definitely feel one of the char- acteristics of brunch is that it's leisurely. It's pretty lovely because we're able to talk, drink coffee, take our time and have a really good, fun conversation and time. And eat a lot of food.' The club, accordingly, seeks out places with good window seats or booths, where they can guarantee a good environment for talking. They will not wait for a seat at the bar.

Though the un-brunch is not yet a fashionable trend that will be written up in all the magazines, some people, in places like Toronto at least, opt for dim sum during weekend brunch-times, a meal as efficient and plentiful as the banquet-hall brunches. Others just go to old-fashioned diners and eat breakfast or lunch without much fuss. But the Portland brunchers and their clubs have been able to maintain their brunching-class identity by enjoying it on their terms and participating in a leisure activity that is actually leisurely.

The Revolution Will Come
with Hollandaise Sauce

The trouble with brunch can be partially overcome when there's
a critical awareness like Portland's Joy Brunch Club has, one
that doesn't in any way preclude fun – awareness of the time it
takes, the social demands it makes and the sometimes ridiculous
things it makes people do. Constraint is a most sublime force,
turning a pastime that is unwieldy into something with a focused
purpose. Leisure time is why we work so hard and is what makes
life worth living, affording us time for religion, family, art, hobbies,
social service and a long list of activities that we hold dear but
that aren't exactly work. Brunch can be a wonderful brief escape
from busy lives, but it doesn't escape some very important things,
like the erosion of what made the middle class so desirable: stability, a good work/life balance and genuine leisure time. The brunching class can correct some of their own activities, Portland-style,
but then use these pursuits and their lifestyle identities to relate
to one another. There are enough overlaps in this identity that
it's strong enough to create a sense of unity through the varied
and sundry work world middle-class people find themselves in
today, a high-risk landscape where the safety net that once existed
is no longer there.

Richard Florida's data shows this is how people identify, and
Farha Ternikar's research into brunch demonstrates lifestyle
connections like this are deeply rooted and are not just local but
global in scope, cutting across cultural, gender and racial lines.
Brunching lifestyles have a reach far beyond what's happening at
a local café, even to places with chaotic recent histories like Buenos
Aires, where the brunching class has appeared among its traditional middle class, people who have clung to their way of life
despite the challenges. The global potential for class consciousness
via lifestyle pursuits seems great. If my hometown's culture
allowed for strong social links and mixing across perceived divides
between union and management, between white collar and blue,
why can't this happen elsewhere? Our work lives no longer have

the obvious commonalities that encourage people to come together and improve their lot, as large groups of people doing industrial jobs no longer exist. The old ways of organizing are incredibly difficult (and they were never easy) when applied to the new economy.

There is resistance to this kind of new class consciousness because it doesn't fit into the established paradigms. More problematically, it hinges on consumerism with a particular kind of connoisseurship that few participants want to admit is actually consumerism but everybody is buying anyway. There are no greater fans of craft beer, farmers' markets, organic yoga mats and heirloom brie than traditional lefties, the same people who colonize formerly working-class neighbourhoods and transform them into Yorkvilles, Upper East Sides and Nob and Notting Hills, even as they make aesthetic claims on the dirtier workaday world they've displaced. These are the very same ones who find hotel brunches and diners uncool, things the working class looked and look to for glamour and utility. Instead of denying an inherent middle-class sensibility, the brunching class need to own it and look at how they live, how they consume and how they work, and recognize the commonalities with other people who do some, but not necessarily all, the same things.

Thorstein Veblen's leisure-loving Victorians became today's creative and professional types, many of whom don't identify as left or right but rather situate themselves in a hazy, somewhat apolitical, centre. The rub is they are all facing the same struggles as people with more politicized views, and brunch and leisure are an opportunity to form an identity across heretofore-disparate segments of this reluctant class. And since class is not tied directly to money, but rather sensibility, there's an opportunity to pull a wide spectrum of incomes into this shared consciousness. Previous generations had company and union loyalty; the equivalent today is lifestyle loyalty.

Through conspicuous consumption, why not conspicuous cohesion? At a time when social cohesion seems to be coming apart, leisure presents a place where shared values can be capitalized on and used for so much more. They can flip the aspirational characteristics of this culture into a clear-eyed view of how wider social good and justice can benefit themselves and others. Authenticity, class and much of how we live is socially constructed, and there's nothing to prevent us from becoming better builders.

As I said at the beginning of this book, an undertaking that has been a process of figuring out what class has meant to me and how to articulate it, I find the middle-class life desirable, and as I continue to slide into this comfortable sensibility, I never want to lose sight of the edge. I want to keep the critical perspective that growing up in Windsor gave me. The fault lines are everywhere, or, as Yeats wrote in 'The Second Coming,' his poem that inspired the title of one of Didion's California essays, 'Things fall apart; the centre cannot hold.' I don't want to become oblivious like Yeats' falcon, unable to hear the falconer as it turned and turned in a widening gyre.

Thomas Frank's book is called *What's the Matter With Kansas?* but this book you're holding could be called *What's the Matter with the Middle Class?* The middle class continues to be in denial of what it is while disregarding the things that are in its best interest to pay attention to. We need more control over our lives. We can't keep giving our time and work away. I fear the crisis will have to get much worse before we are shocked into collective action. I don't have any easy answer as to how to do any of this, but class struggles are always hard work. And we have lots of time to think and talk about this while we're waiting in line for brunch.

Bibliography

Books/Journals

Didion, Joan. *Slouching Towards Bethlehem*. London: Flamingo, 2001.

Florida, Richard. *The Rise of the Creative Class ... and how it's transforming work, leisure, community, & everyday life*. New York: Basic Books, 2004.

Frank, Thomas. *What's the Matter with Kansas? How the Conservatives Won the Heart of America*. New York: Holt Paperbacks, 2005.

McWilliams, James. 'Are Farmers' Markets That Good for Us?' *Freakonomics*. 2009.

Schlichtman, John Joe and Patch, Jason. 'Gentrifier? Who, Me? Interrogating the Gentrifier in the Mirror,' *International Journal of Urban and Regional Research*. 2013.

Veblen, Thorstein. *The Theory of the Leisure Class*. New York: Oxford University Press, 2007.

Woolley, Frances. 'Why politicians court the middle class,' *Worthwhile Canadian Initiative.* 2012.

Reports

'Caught in the Time Crunch: Time Use, Leisure and Culture in Canada,' *Canadian Index of Wellbeing*, University of Waterloo. 2010.

Acknowledgements

Writing about class, personal and otherwise, was more of a challenge than I had imagined. I'm thankful for the long chats I had with friends while trying to get a handle on the sensibilities around the working and middle classes I've bumped into and been a part of. Thanks especially to Anna Bowness, Michelle Kasprzak and Simon Reader for these open and meandering explorations. Others, like Elizabeth Bowie, Jessica Duffin-Wolfe, Todd Irvine, Dale Duncan, Tabatha Southey, Alfred Holden, Stephen Otto and Ivor Tossell were essential cheerleaders along the way. My family deserves credit for their encouragement, and providing a solid place to come from and a clear view of the world. And deepest gratitude to wonderful Robert Ruggiero for unwearyingly coming along on this ride and enduring the ornery harangues of a lost writer. Much love to all these people.

Coach House is a dear place that allowed me considerable room to figure out how to write a book with as vague a premise as 'something about class.' Thanks to Evan Munday for a light bulb moment early on, without which this book would not be. Heidi Waechtler provided tremendous editorial help throughout the production of this manuscript. Stuart Ross's insights and assistance were invaluable in the final stages of production. Alana Wilcox's sharp edits and suggestions were essential to this book, as was an early conversation with her about class and the sometimes fraught journey from small town to big city. Writing this book was a process of discovery, and Jason McBride's skilful shaping of an unwieldy collection of disparate ideas into a coherent narrative let me say things I'd not have been able to say on my own. Much thanks and gratitude to these last two people in particular for their patience and most gentle encouragement.

About the Author

Shawn Micallef (@shawnmicallef) is the author of *Stroll: Psychogeographic Walking Tours of Toronto* and *Full Frontal T.O.*, a weekly columnist at the *Toronto Star*, and a senior editor and co-owner of the independent, Jane Jacobs Prize–winning magazine *Spacing*. Shawn teaches at the University of Toronto and was a 2011–2012 Canadian Journalism Fellow at University of Toronto's Massey College. In 2002, while a resident at the Canadian Film Centre's Media Lab, he co-founded [murmur], the location-based mobile phone documentary project that has spread to over twenty-five cities globally. Shawn was the Toronto Public Library's Writer in Residence in fall 2013.

About the
Exploded Views Series

Exploded Views is a series of probing, provocative essays that offer surprising perspectives on the most intriguing cultural issues and figures of our day. Longer than a typical magazine article but shorter than a full-length book, these are punchy salvos written by some of North America's most lyrical journalists and critics. Spanning a variety of forms and genres – history, biography, polemic, commentary – and published simultaneously in all digital formats and handsome, collectible print editions, this is literary reportage that at once investigates, illuminates and intervenes.

www.chbooks.com/explodedviews

Typeset in Goodchild Pro and Gibson Pro. Goodchild was designed by Nick Shinn in 2002 at his ShinnType foundry in Orangeville, Ontario. Shinn's design takes its inspiration from French printer Nicholas Jenson who, at the height of the Renaissance in Venice, used the basic Carolingian minuscule calligraphic hand and classic roman inscriptional capitals to arrive at a typeface that produced a clear and even texture that most literate Europeans could read. Shinn's design captures the calligraphic feel of Jensen's early types in a more refined digital format. Gibson was designed by Rod McDonald in honour of John Gibson FGDC (1928–2011), Rod's long-time friend and one of the founders of the Society of Graphic Designers of Canada. It was McDonald's intention to design a solid, contemporary and affordable sans serif face.

Printed at the old Coach House on bpNichol Lane in Toronto, Ontario, on Rolland Opaque Natural paper, which was manufactured, acid-free, in Saint-Jérôme, Quebec, from 50 percent recycled paper, and it was printed with vegetable-based ink on a 1965 Heidelberg KORD offset litho press. Its pages were folded on a Baumfolder, gathered by hand, bound on a Sulby Auto-Minabinda and trimmed on a Polar single-knife cutter.

Edited by Jason McBride
Copy edited by Stuart Ross
Designed by Alana Wilcox
Series cover design by Ingrid Paulson
Cover photo by Elizabeth Sullivan
Author photo by Beth Darbyshire

Coach House Books
80 bpNichol Lane
Toronto ON M5S 3J4
Canada

416 979 2217
800 367 6360

mail@chbooks.com
www.chbooks.com